A IS I
FRIEND
ONLY IF

JAMIR IBRAHIM SHAIKH

AI IS FRIEND ONLY IF ...

By

JAMIR IBRAHIM SHAIKH

AI IS FRIEND ONLY IF ... By JAMIR IBRAHIM SHAIKH

First published in England by
SIFAR INTERNATIONAL PUBLICATION

Near Markfield Conference Centre,
Gatsby Lane, Markfield, Leicester,
LE67 9SY United Kingdom

E-mail:EbooksSifar@gmail.com

Cover
iMPRESSION GRAPHICS
WeMakeImpression@gmail.com

Cataloguing in-Publication Data is available from the
British Library

ISBN 9798883063403

Price: 19.99 USD

What AI Head, Former Senior Data security at NIIA say

"Real life working and actual data helps you to take decisions faster and stay ahead of The Others!"

" It always helped us while working for security measures forcountry's top decorated people...

This is the only **KEY** to the **RICHEST** that is easy, important and achievable for a common man!

Kindly check both the books. This one and the one mentioned below if you want to choose Best AI Company to invest.

Early the fastest is proved when Stock market is a major concern

This first book shall introduce you to the fascinating world of A.I and what its all about in common man's terms.

Make you aware about true or false fears of artificial intelligence. It also deals with the the Myths and Myths busted, gives lot of examples in order to take advantage ethically of this great technological tornado.

Second book which is here –

>> Click here to know AI Future Ahead – 2032 <<

Throws the light on very important and crucial data which in my view very very costly if one needs to buy it in accordance with stock market of AI Product companies.

Many of us have missed the Bitcoin wave and repenting till now….

But here is the chance to ride another wealth wave called Artificial intelligence … and companies promoting its products!!

- *William James*
  (AI Head, Former Senior Data security at NIA)

>> Click here to know AI Future Ahead – 2032 <<

ALL THE BEST

ın order to Invest in the Right AI Company

- A Global Perspective on REAL Statistical data, Trends, and Future Growth

>> Click here to know AI Future Ahead – 2032 <<

PEOPLE lost the best opportunity to make money in the BITCOIN WAVE

BUT

With the help of this ebook, you shall ride the bigger wave than Bitcoin for sure.

>> https://www.amazon.com/dp/B0CVFBBK85 <<

- *William James*
  (AI Head, Former Senior Data security at NIA)

TABLE OF CONTENTS

10 negative propaganda about AI today?

Everyone is curious as well scared by thinking about this new thing in technology called AI – aka Artificial intelligence!

It happened every time in history, when something new is coming to change the way technology work, the fear of losing jobs, ethical concerns, political influences, etc,. are always discussed.

Beneficial to humanity factors are always won if you look back into any world history when such things have happened.

Let the helpful factors win at the end in this new turmoil too!

It's important to note that the following points are not facts but fictional negative propaganda.

While AI technology has tremendous potential benefits, ethical considerations and responsible development are crucial to address any concerns.

So let's dive into this new great thing and find out why is it great and how shall it help humanity and make our life easier that before?

Below are the most 10 negative propaganda about AI today

AI as Job Destroyer:

Propaganda suggests that AI is ruthlessly replacing human jobs, leading to mass unemployment and economic instability. This narrative ignores the potential for AI to create new job opportunities and enhance existing roles.

AI Control over Humanity:

Misinformation alleges that AI is on a path to gain absolute control over human society, portraying a dystopian future where machines manipulate and dominate human decision-making.

Surveillance State Powered by AI:

Unfounded claims paint AI as a tool for totalitarian surveillance, arguing that governments and corporations use advanced AI to spy on citizens, eroding personal privacy rights.

AI-Induced Inequality:

Propaganda suggests that AI exacerbates societal inequality by favoring the wealthy and powerful. This narrative ignores the potential for AI to address societal challenges and bridge gaps through equitable applications.

AI as a Threat to Democracy:

Unsubstantiated claims contend that AI poses a direct threat to democratic processes, suggesting that advanced algorithms can be manipulated to influence elections and undermine democratic values.

AI Discrimination and Bias:

Propaganda highlights instances of AI bias and discrimination, exaggerating isolated incidents to create a narrative that AI systematically perpetuates unfair treatment, particularly towards marginalized communities.

AI as a Source of Unemployment:

False narratives suggest that AI's rise leads to wide spread unemployment, overlooking the potential for AI to augment human capabilities, create new job sectors, and enhance productivity.

AI Malfunctions as Catastrophes:

Sensationalized stories depict AI systems as ticking time bombs, ready to malfunction catastrophically and cause widespread disasters, fostering fear without acknowledging rigorous safety measures in place.

AI as an Existential Threat:

Unfounded claims portray AI as an imminent existential threat, warning of a future where machines surpass human intelligence and pose an apocalyptic risk to humanity.

AI Inability to Understand Human Emotions:

Propaganda misrepresents AI's capabilities, suggesting that AI lacks the ability to understand human emotions, leading to the false idea that it is incapable of empathetic or ethical decision-making.

It is very essential to approach discussions about AI with a critical mindset, separating fact from fiction, and promoting responsible discourse around the ethical development and deployment of AI technologies.

How the Myths be solved?

What are the highest qualitative and best solutions to solve these myths?

Addressing myths and misconceptions surrounding AI requires a multifaceted and comprehensive approach. Here are key strategies to counteract these myths and promote a more accurate understanding of AI:

Education and Awareness:

Invest in educational initiatives that provide accurate information about AI. Foster awareness programs targeting various demographics, including the general public, policymakers, and professionals. This can involve workshops, seminars, and online courses to dispel myths and increase understanding.

Transparent Communication:

Promote transparency in AI development and applications. Encourage companies and developers to communicate openly about their AI systems, sharing information about how algorithms work, potential biases, and the ethical considerations taken into account during development.

Responsible Journalism:

Encourage responsible reporting by media outlets. Journalists play a pivotal role in shaping public perception. By emphasizing accuracy, context, and the positive aspects of AI, media can contribute to a more informed public discourse.

Collaboration with Stakeholders:

Foster collaboration among stakeholders, including industry leaders, policymakers, ethicists, and the public. Engage in open discussions about AI's benefits and challenges, ensuring diverse perspectives are considered in the development and deployment of AI technologies.

Regulatory Frameworks:

Establish and update regulatory frameworks that govern AI development. Ensure that these frameworks address ethical considerations, fairness, accountability, and transparency. Collaborate internationally to create consistent standards that guide responsible AI practices globally.

Promote Ethical AI Development:

Encourage developers to adopt ethical AI practices. Emphasize the importance of fair and unbiased algorithms, privacy protection, and responsible data usage. Provide guidelines and best practices for incorporating ethical considerations into the design and deployment of AI systems.

Highlight Positive Use Cases:

Showcase real-world examples of positive AI applications. Highlight instances where AI has contributed to solving complex problems, improving efficiency, and benefiting society. Positive use cases help counterbalance negative narratives.

Public Engagement:

Engage the public in discussions about AI. Solicit input on AI applications and policies, and address concerns through transparent communication. By involving the public, you create a more inclusive and democratic approach to AI development.

Addressing Bias and Discrimination:

Actively work to address biases in AI algorithms. Implement measures to detect and mitigate biases, and promote fairness in AI systems. Research and development efforts should focus on creating more inclusive and unbiased algorithms.

Human-AI Collaboration:

Emphasize the concept of human-AI collaboration rather than a stark replacement of human jobs. Highlight the ways in which AI can augment human capabilities, leading to enhanced productivity, creativity, and problem-solving.

By implementing these strategies, there can be a concerted effort to dispel myths, foster a more accurate understanding of AI, and ensure that the development and deployment of AI technologies align with ethical considerations and benefit humanity at large. Education, collaboration, and ethical practices are essential components of building a positive narrative around AI.

Medical Diagnostics with AI Imaging:

should focus on creating more inclusive and unbiased algorithms.

Human-AI Collaboration:

Emphasize the concept of human-AI collaboration rather than a stark replacement of human jobs. Highlight the ways in which AI can augment human capabilities, leading to enhanced productivity, creativity, and problem-solving.

By implementing these strategies, there can be a concerted effort to dispel myths, foster a more accurate understanding of AI, and ensure that the development and deployment of AI technologies align with ethical considerations and benefit humanity at large. Education, collaboration, and ethical practices are essential components of building a positive narrative around AI.

Medical Diagnostics with AI Imaging:

Highlight Positive Use Cases:

Showcase real-world examples of positive AI applications. Highlight instances where AI has contributed to solving complex problems, improving efficiency, and benefiting society. Positive use cases help counterbalance negative narratives.

Public Engagement:

Engage the public in discussions about AI. Solicit input on AI applications and policies, and address concerns through transparent communication. By involving the public, you create a more inclusive and democratic approach to AI development.

Addressing Bias and Discrimination:

Actively work to address biases in AI algorithms. Implement measures to detect and mitigate biases, and promote fairness in AI systems. Research and development efforts

Human-AI collaboration is revolutionizing medical diagnostics, especially in radiology. AI algorithms assist radiologists in interpreting medical images, providing faster and more accurate diagnoses. This collaborative approach enhances the efficiency of healthcare professionals and improves patient outcomes.

AI-Augmented Creativity in Art and Design:

Artists and designers are leveraging AI tools to enhance their creative processes. AI algorithms can generate unique patterns, suggest color palettes, and even contribute to the design of digital or physical artwork. This collaboration between human creativity and AI innovation leads to novel and inspiring artistic expressions.

AI-Powered Content Creation:

Content creators, including writers and journalists, collaborate with AI tools to streamline the content creation process. AI algorithms assist in generating ideas, summarizing information, and even drafting initial versions of articles. Human editors then refine and add the nuanced touch that reflects human creativity and perspective.

Customer Service – Chat bots:

Chat-bots powered by AI are employed in customer service to handle routine queries and provide instant responses. While chatbots handle common inquiries, human agents can focus on more complex and emotionally nuanced interactions, creating a seamless and efficient customer service experience.

Manufacturing and Robotics:

In manufacturing, AI-powered robots collaborate with human workers to improve efficiency and safety. Robots handle repetitive or dangerous tasks, allowing humans to focus on more complex aspects of production, quality control, and problem-solving.

Financial Decision-Making with AI:

Financial analysts collaborate with AI algorithms to analyze vast datasets and identify trends in the stock market. AI tools can provide data-driven insights, while human experts use their judgment, experience, and market knowledge to make informed investment decisions.

AI-Assisted Language Translation:

Language translation services are enhanced by AI, enabling faster and more accurate translations. Human translators collaborate with AI tools to handle large volumes of content efficiently, ensuring that translations maintain cultural nuances and linguistic intricacies.

Personalized Learning in Education:

AI is transforming education by tailoring learning experiences to individual students. Educational platforms use AI algorithms to analyze student performance and adapt content to suit their learning styles. Teachers then leverage this data to provide targeted support and guidance.

Collaborative Design in Architecture:

Architects and designers collaborate with AI tools to optimize building designs. AI algorithms can analyze various parameters, such as energy efficiency and structural integrity, while architects bring their creative vision and understanding of human needs to create innovative and sustainable structures.

AI in Scientific Research:

Scientists collaborate with AI to accelerate research processes. AI algorithms analyze vast datasets, identify patterns, and suggest potential hypotheses. Researchers then validate and interpret the results, leveraging AI as a powerful tool for data-driven scientific discovery.

These examples demonstrate how Human-AI collaboration can lead to synergies that enhance productivity, creativity, and problem-solving across various domains. The combination of human intuition, creativity, and emotional intelligence with AI's analytical power can unlock new possibilities and drive positive advancements in multiple fields.

Unleashing the Power of AI

A Case Study on its Best Advantage to Humans

Artificial Intelligence (AI) has emerged as a transformative force, reshaping the way we live, work, and interact. In this case study, we delve into the myriad ways AI has become one of the most advantageous tools for humanity. From revolutionizing healthcare to optimizing business operations, AI's impact is profound and far-reaching.

Healthcare Revolution:

Predicting and Preventing Diseases

One of the most significant advantages of AI lies in its application to healthcare. AI-powered predictive analytics has proven to be a game-changer in disease prevention and management. Take, for example, the collaboration between AI and healthcare professionals at a leading medical institution.

Scenario:

A hospital integrated AI algorithms into its systems to analyze patient data, medical records, and genetic information. The goal was to predict the likelihood of chronic diseases such as diabetes and heart conditions in patients.

Implementation:

The AI system processed vast amounts of patient data, identifying patterns and risk factors associated with specific diseases. It could predict the probability of an individual developing a certain condition based on their genetic predisposition, lifestyle, and medical history.

Results:

As a result, healthcare professionals could proactively engage with high-risk patients, offering personalized preventive measures. This approach significantly reduced the incidence of chronic diseases, improved patient outcomes, and lowered overall healthcare costs.

Enhancing Customer Experience: AI in E-commerce

The integration of AI into the e-commerce sector has led to a personalized and seamless shopping experience for consumers. A case study from a prominent online retailer illustrates the impact of AI on enhancing customer satisfaction.

Scenario:

An e-commerce platform sought to improve customer engagement and increase sales by providing tailored product recommendations.

Implementation:

The platform implemented AI algorithms that analyzed user behavior, purchase history, and preferences. These algorithms continuously learned and adapted to individual customer preferences in real-time.

Results:

Customers experienced a more personalized shopping journey with product recommendations that resonated with their tastes. The AI-driven system not only increased sales but also fostered customer loyalty, as users felt a deeper connection with the platform.

Optimizing Energy Consumption: AI in Smart Grids

The energy sector has witnessed substantial benefits from the integration of AI, particularly in the development of smart grids. A case study from a utility company demonstrates how AI optimizes energy consumption and improves grid efficiency.

Scenario:

A utility company aimed to enhance the efficiency of its energy distribution network and reduce energy wastage.

Implementation:

The company deployed AI algorithms to analyze data from sensors, smart meters, and historical usage patterns. The AI system dynamically adjusted energy distribution, predicting demand fluctuations and optimizing the grid in real-time.

Results:

The implementation of AI in the smart grid reduced energy losses, improved overall grid reliability, and lowered operational costs.

Consumers experienced more stable energy supply, and the utility company achieved sustainability goals by minimizing its environmental impact.

Personalized Learning in Education: AI in Online Education Platforms

AI's ability to personalize learning experiences has transformed the education sector. A case study focusing on an online education platform illustrates how AI enhances the learning journey for students worldwide.

Scenario:

An online education platform sought to address the diverse learning needs of students and improve overall engagement.

Implementation:

The platform integrated AI algorithms that analyzed student performance, learning styles, and interactions with course content. The AI system adapted the curriculum in real-time, providing personalized learning paths for each student.

Results:

Students experienced a more tailored and effective learning experience, with AI adapting to their individual strengths and weaknesses. This approach improved overall student performance, retention rates, and satisfaction with the educational platform.

AI in Disaster Response: Enhancing Emergency Services

The use of AI in disaster response has become a critical advantage in managing and mitigating the impact of natural disasters. A case study from an emergency services agency showcases how AI improves response times and resource allocation.

Scenario:

An emergency services agency aimed to enhance its ability to respond swiftly and effectively to natural disasters such as hurricanes and wildfires.

Implementation:

The agency implemented AI-powered predictive models that analyzed weather patterns, satellite imagery, and historical data to anticipate the severity and trajectory of disasters. AI algorithms also optimized resource allocation and evacuation routes.

Results:

The integration of AI significantly improved the agency's ability to predict and respond to disasters, saving lives and minimizing property damage. Real-time data analysis allowed for more informed decision-making during critical moments.

Conclusion:

This case study provides a glimpse into the transformative power of AI across diverse sectors. From revolutionizing healthcare to optimizing energy consumption and enhancing educational experiences, AI has become a cornerstone of human progress. The examples presented demonstrate not only the efficiency gains and cost savings but also the profound positive impact on individuals' lives.

As we move forward, the continuous exploration and ethical implementation of AI technologies hold the promise of even greater advancements. It is crucial for society, academia, and industry to collaborate in harnessing AI's potential while ensuring responsible and ethical development. The case studies presented here serve as beacons of inspiration, showcasing the incredible benefits that AI can bring to humanity when leveraged thoughtfully and with a commitment to improving the human experience.

"Artificial Intelligence Unveiled: A Journey through the Pros and Cons"

In the rapidly evolving landscape of technology, Artificial Intelligence stands as a groundbreaking force that has permeated every aspect of our lives. From enhancing efficiency to raising ethical concerns, this book, "Artificial Intelligence Unveiled: A Journey through the Pros and Cons," delves deep into the heart of AI. Let's embark on a comprehensive exploration, navigating the complexities and potential of this revolutionary technology.

With each chapter, we will unravel the mysteries of AI, breaking down complex concepts into easily digestible information. From its humble beginnings to its transformative applications, we will weigh the benefits against the risks, offering insights that empower readers to make informed decisions about the role of AI in our world.

Hence we have seen so far – AI - is the simulation of human intelligence in machines that are programmed to think and learn. In this introductory chapter, we'll explore the roots of AI, its evolution, and the fundamental principles that govern its functionality.

As we embark on this journey, we'll demystify the terminology and provide a clear understanding of what constitutes artificial intelligence. From the earliest concepts to the modern-day applications, readers will gain a solid foundation to appreciate the significance of AI in our contemporary world.

The Beginnings: Early Developments and Concepts

To truly comprehend the power of Artificial Intelligence, we must delve into its historical origins. In this chapter, we embark on a journey through time, exploring the birth and evolution of AI concepts.

The seeds of AI were sown in the mid-20th century, where pioneers envisioned machines that could mimic human intelligence. We'll encounter iconic figures like Alan Turing and John McCarthy, who laid the foundation for AI research. Turing's groundbreaking ideas about machine intelligence and McCarthy's coining of the term "Artificial Intelligence" set the stage for the subsequent decades of exploration.

Moving forward, we'll explore early AI applications, from simple logic-based systems to the advent of neural networks. The excitement and optimism of the early days of AI research will be palpable, offering readers a glimpse into the enthusiasm that fueled its development.

However, it's crucial to acknowledge the initial challenges and setbacks. As we progress through this chapter, we'll navigate the obstacles faced by early AI researchers, providing a nuanced understanding of the trial-and-error process that led to the birth of intelligent machines.

By the end of this chapter, readers will have a historical context that enables them to appreciate the sheer magnitude of progress AI has undergone. The foundation laid by early pioneers serves as a testament to human ingenuity and the relentless pursuit of creating machines that can think.

AI - The Beginnings: Early Developments and Concepts

The dawn of Artificial Intelligence (AI) witnessed the convergence of human ingenuity and technological ambition. In this chapter, we embark on a captivating journey through the historical roots of AI, exploring the early developments and fundamental concepts that laid the groundwork for the transformative force we know today.

As the mid-20th century unfolded, a visionary group of thinkers began pondering the possibility of creating machines that could emulate human intelligence. Alan Turing, a trailblazer in the field, introduced the concept of a machine capable of mimicking any human's thought process – a concept that would become foundational in AI development. John McCarthy's coining of the term "Artificial Intelligence" crystallized the ambition, setting the stage for a revolution in computing.

The Evolutionary Tapestry:

Our exploration continues with an in-depth look at the early AI applications that emerged from these groundbreaking ideas. Logic-based systems, a rudimentary form of AI, were among the first attempts to replicate human decision-making in machines. This era marked the experimental phase, where theorists and engineers grappled with the complexities of creating intelligent systems.

Neural networks, inspired by the human brain's structure, began to take center stage in AI research. The mid-section of this chapter delves into the intricacies of early neural network models and their attempts to simulate human learning processes. As we navigate this terrain, we encounter both the triumphs and tribulations faced by pioneers who sought to imbue machines with cognitive abilities.

The journey through the mid-section extends to the birth of expert systems, designed to replicate the decision-making prowess of human experts in specific domains. We explore how these early endeavors paved the way for machine learning, a paradigm shift that would redefine the landscape of AI. The chapter unfolds as a narrative of relentless experimentation, fueled by an unyielding desire to create intelligent machines.

Navigating Challenges and Setbacks:

No historical exploration is complete without acknowledging the challenges faced along the way. The mid-20th century was marked by periods of optimism and frustration as early AI researchers confronted computational limitations and conceptual roadblocks. We dissect the setbacks, from the initial struggles with computing power to the realization that true machine intelligence demanded more than mere algorithmic instructions.

Yet, even in the face of challenges, the visionaries persevered. The mid-section of this chapter illuminates the resilience and determination that characterized the early AI community. It's a tale of learning from failures, refining approaches, and inching closer to the elusive goal of artificial intelligence.

As we conclude this chapter, we stand at the crossroads of history, witnessing the birth pangs of a technological revolution. The beginnings of AI were marked by audacity, curiosity, and an unshakeable belief in the possibility of machines mirroring human intelligence.

The chapter encapsulates the gestation period of AI, where visionary ideas collided with the practicalities of implementation. From Turing's theoretical constructs to the emergence of neural networks and expert systems, each step laid the foundation for the next, forming a continuum of progress.

In the next chapter, we will build upon this historical backdrop, delving into the core principles that govern how AI works. The journey through the beginnings has set the stage for a deeper understanding of the complexities that define artificial intelligence. As we turn the page, the excitement of early discoveries paves the way for a more profound exploration of AI's inner workings.

How AI Works: Understanding the Basics

In the enigmatic realm of Artificial Intelligence (AI), understanding how machines replicate human intelligence is crucial. "How AI Works: Understanding the Basics," unravels the intricacies of AI processes. As we delve into this chapter, we embark on a journey to demystify the core principles governing the functionality of AI systems.

AI's modus operandi revolves around the assimilation of data, learning from it, and making decisions akin to human cognition. This chapter elucidates the fundamental building blocks that constitute the backbone of AI, ensuring readers gain a comprehensive grasp of the inner workings.

The Cognitive Machinery:

The mid-section of this chapter immerses us in the anatomy of AI algorithms. At its core, AI functions through intricate algorithms designed laid the foundation for the next, forming a continuum of progress.

In the next chapter, we will build upon this historical backdrop, delving into the core principles that govern how AI works. The journey through the beginnings has set the stage for a deeper understanding of the complexities that define artificial intelligence. As we turn the page, the excitement of early discoveries paves the way for a more profound exploration of AI's inner workings.

How AI Works: Understanding the Basics

In the enigmatic realm of Artificial Intelligence (AI), understanding how machines replicate human intelligence is crucial. "How AI Works: Understanding the Basics," unravels the intricacies of AI processes. As we delve into this chapter, we embark on a journey to demystify the core principles governing the functionality of AI systems.

AI's modus operandi revolves around the assimilation of data, learning from it, and making decisions akin to human cognition. This chapter elucidates the fundamental building blocks that constitute the backbone of AI, ensuring readers gain a comprehensive grasp of the inner workings.

The Cognitive Machinery:

The mid-section of this chapter immerses us in the anatomy of AI algorithms. At its core, AI functions through intricate algorithms designed

Data: The Lifeblood of AI:

The heartbeat of AI lies in its ability to ingest, process, and interpret vast amounts of data. The mid-section extends its focus to the pivotal role of data in AI functionality. From structured to unstructured data, the chapter elucidates how AI algorithms sift through information, discern patterns, and make informed decisions.

The concept of feature engineering is unraveled, showcasing the art of selecting and transforming raw data into meaningful inputs for AI models. This chapter underscores the symbiotic relationship between data quality and AI performance, emphasizing the criticality of meticulous data curation.

As we conclude our exploration into the intricacies of AI functionality, a profound understanding of its basics emerges. AI is not an arcane force but a structured amalgamation of algorithms, data, and learning processes. The chapter serves as a compass, guiding to process and interpret data. We explore the foundational concepts of machine learning, a paradigm where AI systems learn patterns and make predictions without explicit programming.

Supervised learning, unsupervised learning, and reinforcement learning are dissected to unveil their distinct roles in shaping AI intelligence. We traverse through real-world examples, illustrating how algorithms learn from labeled datasets, discover patterns autonomously, and refine their decision-making through continuous feedback.

To comprehend the essence of AI, it's imperative to grasp the significance of neural networks. The mid-section delves into the neural architecture, mirroring the human brain's interconnected neurons. As we unravel the layers of neural networks, we uncover their role in image and speech recognition, natural language processing, and other complex tasks.

readers through the labyrinth of machine intelligence.

The cognitive machinery, fueled by algorithms and neural networks, propels AI to unprecedented heights. The realization that data is the lifeblood of AI underscores its voracious appetite for information, a hunger that drives continuous learning and adaptation.

In the upcoming chapters, we will apply this foundational knowledge to explore AI's real-world applications, from transforming daily life to revolutionizing industries. The journey through the basics has equipped us with the tools to appreciate the symbiotic relationship between AI and data, laying the groundwork for a deeper exploration of its impact on our evolving world.

Applications that Transform: AI in Everyday Life

In an era where technology has become synonymous with daily existence, Chapter 4 unravels the profound impact of Artificial Intelligence (AI) on the very fabric of our lives. "Applications that Transform: AI in Everyday Life" guides readers through an immersive exploration of how AI seamlessly integrates into the rhythms of our daily existence.

This chapter seeks to peel back the layers of AI's influence, revealing a world where innovation is not confined to laboratories but thrives in our homes, workplaces, and social interactions. AI, once a futuristic concept, is now a tangible force, reshaping how we navigate our mornings, conduct business, and communicate with one another.

The Morning Routine: AI at Home

As the sun rises, we step into a realm where AI has become an unseen but indispensable household assistant. Smart homes, equipped with AI-driven devices, showcase a level of automation that not only simplifies tasks but also anticipates our needs. From adjusting room temperatures to brewing coffee with precision, these AI applications create an environment that adapts to our preferences.

Virtual assistants, powered by sophisticated AI algorithms, serve as personalized concierges, providing weather updates, traffic predictions, and tailored news. The mid-section of this chapter explores how these virtual companions not only make our mornings more efficient but also contribute to the growing synergy between human lifestyles and artificial intelligence.

The Workday Revolution: AI in Business

Stepping out into the bustling world of business, we witness a revolutionary transformation driven by AI applications. The mid-section navigates through the intricate web of AI's impact on various aspects of the corporate landscape. Intelligent data analytics emerges as a guiding force, offering businesses insights that drive informed decision-making and strategic planning.

Automation takes center stage as routine tasks are seamlessly executed by AI, freeing up human resources for more creative and strategic endeavors. Chatbots and virtual assistants, woven into the fabric of corporate communication, streamline interactions, enhance customer service, and contribute to a more agile and responsive business ecosystem.

The Social Sphere: AI in Communication

As the day unfolds, our journey through AI's applications extends to the social sphere, where communication is reshaped by intelligent algorithms. Social media platforms leverage AI to curate personalized content, presenting users with information tailored to their preferences. The mid-section delves into the intricate world of AI-driven content targeting and advertisement placement, showcasing the symbiotic relationship between users and the algorithms that understand their preferences.

Facial recognition technology, an awe-inspiring achievement of AI, finds applications in photo tagging, security systems, and even emotion detection. This segment explores the implications of such technology, raising important questions about the balance between convenience and privacy, and the ethical considerations associated with AI in communication.

As we wrap up our exploration of AI's transformative applications in everyday life, a panoramic view emerges. AI, once confined to the realms of science fiction, is now an omnipresent force subtly shaping our existence. From the intimate spaces of our homes to the dynamic landscapes of businesses and the interconnected realm of social communication, AI is not just a tool; it is a transformative companion.

The applications we've explored in this chapter merely scratch the surface of AI's potential. The morning routine showcased AI's ability to enhance domestic comfort, the workday revolution highlighted its role as a catalyst for business evolution, and the social sphere underscored the delicate interplay between technological advancement and ethical considerations.

As we move forward into subsequent chapters, this groundwork of understanding AI's presence in our daily lives becomes the canvas upon which we'll paint a more detailed portrait of its benefits, pitfalls, and ethical considerations. The transformative applications of AI serve as an invitation to delve deeper into the complex interplay between technology and humanity.

The Bright Side: Benefits of Artificial Intelligence

As we navigate the landscape of Artificial Intelligence (AI), "The Bright Side: Benefits of Artificial Intelligence," illuminates the positive facets of this transformative technology. Beyond the algorithms and data, AI stands as a beacon of innovation, offering a multitude of benefits that touch every aspect of our lives.

This chapter embarks on a journey to explore the ways in which AI enhances efficiency, fosters innovation, and brings about positive societal changes. It serves as a counterpoint to apprehensions, focusing on the tremendous advantages that AI brings to the table. From healthcare to education, businesses to scientific research, the bright side of AI reveals a tapestry of positive transformations.

Empowering Healthcare:

The mid-section of this chapter delves into one of the most significant arenas where AI shines — healthcare. AI applications have revolutionized diagnostics, offering more accurate and faster analyses of medical images, such as X-rays and MRIs. The precision and efficiency of AI-driven diagnostics not only accelerate the decision-making process for healthcare professionals but also contribute to early detection and treatment.

Beyond diagnostics, AI aids in personalized medicine, tailoring treatment plans based on individual patient data. Predictive analytics, empowered by AI, assists in forecasting disease outbreaks, optimizing resource allocation, and improving overall public health management. The transformative impact of AI in healthcare promises a future where medical interventions are more precise, accessible, and timely.

Catalyzing Scientific Discovery:

Moving forward, the mid-section explores the invaluable contributions of AI in scientific research. The ability of AI to process massive datasets and identify patterns accelerates the pace of scientific discovery. In fields such as genomics, AI algorithms analyze genetic data, unlocking insights into complex biological processes and contributing to advancements in personalized medicine.

Simulation and modeling, powered by AI, enable researchers to explore complex phenomena, from climate patterns to subatomic particle interactions. The chapter illuminates how AI acts as a catalyst for breakthroughs, fostering interdisciplinary collaboration and pushing the boundaries of what we can understand and achieve in the realm of science.

Enhancing Education:

The transformative influence of AI extends to the realm of education, forming the focus of the next segment. AI-driven educational technologies personalize learning experiences, adapting to individual student needs and providing targeted feedback. Intelligent tutoring systems, virtual classrooms, and interactive educational content redefine traditional teaching methods, fostering a more inclusive and adaptive learning environment.

Moreover, AI plays a pivotal role in automating administrative tasks, allowing educators to focus more on personalized interaction with students. This chapter segment underscores how AI is not just a tool for efficiency but a partner in cultivating a generation of learners equipped with skills for the future.

As we conclude our exploration of the bright side of AI, a resounding narrative emerges — AI is a force for positive transformation. From healthcare to scientific research and education, the benefits of AI extend beyond mere convenience; they reshape the very foundations of these domains.

The healthcare sector witnesses a paradigm shift, with AI contributing to quicker and more accurate diagnostics, personalized treatments, and improved public health management. In scientific research, AI acts as an accelerant, propelling us into new frontiers of understanding. In education, AI becomes an adaptive ally, tailoring learning experiences to individual needs and paving the way for a more inclusive and dynamic educational landscape.

This chapter serves as a testament to the potential of AI to enhance human capabilities, solve complex problems, and contribute to the betterment of society. As we continue our journey through the multifaceted world of AI, the bright side highlighted in this chapter serves as a foundation for understanding the nuanced interplay between technological innovation and the collective well-being of humanity.

50 examples of what AI can do and what human can not

Image Recognition: AI can analyze and identify objects, faces, and patterns in images more swiftly than humans.

Language Translation: AI-powered language translation tools can quickly and accurately translate text between multiple languages, surpassing human speed and precision.

Medical Diagnostics: AI algorithms can analyze medical images and data to diagnose diseases with a high level of accuracy, often exceeding human capabilities.

Predictive Analytics: AI can process vast amounts of data to predict trends, behaviors, and outcomes, providing valuable insights for decision-making.

Autonomous Vehicles: AI enables self-driving cars to navigate complex environments, making split-second decisions based on real-time data.

Speech Recognition: AI-driven systems can transcribe spoken words with high accuracy, facilitating voice commands and transcription services.

Fraud Detection: AI can detect patterns indicative of fraudulent activities in financial transactions more efficiently than traditional methods.

Weather Forecasting: AI models can process extensive weather data to generate accurate and timely forecasts, surpassing human capability for data analysis.

Game Strategies: AI algorithms can master complex games like chess and Go, often surpassing human champions in strategic thinking.

Personalized Content Recommendations: AI algorithms analyze user preferences to provide tailored content recommendations in entertainment, news, and shopping.

Humanoid Robotics: AI-driven humanoid robots can perform tasks in environments unsafe for humans, such as disaster response or exploration.

Virtual Assistants: AI-powered virtual assistants, like Siri or Alexa, can understand and respond to natural language queries, facilitating hands-free interaction.

Stock Market Trading: AI algorithms can analyze market trends and execute trades at speeds impossible for humans, optimizing investment strategies.

Drug Discovery: AI accelerates the drug discovery process by analyzing biological data, predicting potential drug candidates, and optimizing molecular structures.

Customer Support Chat-bots: AI-powered chatbots provide instant and accurate responses to customer inquiries, improving efficiency in customer support.

Predicting Disease Outbreaks: AI can analyze global health data to predict and monitor the spread of diseases, aiding in early intervention.

Automated Content Creation: AI can generate creative content, including writing articles, composing music, and creating visual art.

Facial Recognition: AI algorithms can accurately identify and verify individuals through facial features, enhancing security systems.

Language Generation: AI models like OpenAI's GPT-3 can generate human-like text based on prompts, demonstrating a form of creative language use.

Automated Code Generation: AI can assist in writing and optimizing code, automating repetitive programming tasks.

Cyber-security: AI enhances cybersecurity by detecting and preventing cyber threats through real-time analysis of network traffic and behaviors.

E-commerce Personalization: AI analyzes user behavior to recommend products, personalize shopping experiences, and optimize pricing strategies.

Emotion Recognition: AI can analyze facial expressions and voice tone to detect emotions, aiding in customer feedback analysis and mental health applications.

Humanoid Customer Service Robots: AI-powered robots can assist customers in retail environments, providing information and assistance.

Supply Chain Optimization: AI algorithms optimize supply chain processes, predicting demand, reducing costs, and improving efficiency.

Text Summarization: AI can summarize lengthy texts, extracting key information and providing concise overviews.

Robotic Process Automation: AI automates routine and rule-based tasks in business processes, improving efficiency and reducing errors.

AI in Agriculture: AI applications analyze data from sensors, satellites, and drones to optimize crop management, pest control, and irrigation.

Biometric Security: AI enhances biometric authentication systems, such as fingerprint or iris recognition, ensuring secure access.

Natural Disaster Prediction: AI analyzes geological and meteorological data to predict and mitigate the impact of natural disasters.

AI in Education: AI facilitates personalized learning, adapts curriculum to individual needs, and provides intelligent tutoring.

Sentiment Analysis: AI algorithms can analyze social media and customer feedback to gauge public sentiment about products, services, or events.

Autonomous Drones: AI enables drones to navigate and perform tasks autonomously, from surveillance to package delivery.

Energy Consumption Optimization: AI optimizes energy usage in buildings and industries, reducing waste and environmental impact.

Medical Chat-bots: AI-powered chat-bots assist in providing preliminary medical advice, symptom analysis, and appointment scheduling.

Sports Analytics: AI processes vast amounts of sports data for performance analysis, injury prevention, and strategic decision-making.

AI in Music Composition: AI models can compose music, creating original pieces based on specific styles or genres.

Virtual Reality (VR) and Augmented Reality (AR): AI enhances immersive experiences in VR and AR applications, adapting content based on user interactions.

Smart Home Automation: AI systems automate and optimize home functions, from temperature control to security, based on user preferences and habits.

Autonomous Underwater Vehicles: AI enables underwater drones to navigate ocean environments for research, exploration, and environmental monitoring.

AI Journalism: AI algorithms can analyze data and generate news articles, providing automated reporting on certain topics.

Laboratory Automation: AI robots assist in laboratory tasks, from conducting experiments to analyzing results, accelerating scientific research.

Elderly Care Robotics: AI-powered robots provide companionship and assistance to the elderly, monitoring health and well-being.

AI in Architecture: AI aids in architectural design, optimizing building layouts, energy efficiency, and environmental impact.

AI-driven Accessibility Tools: AI applications enhance accessibility for individuals with disabilities, providing features like speech-to-text and text-to-speech.

Smart Traffic Management: AI optimizes traffic flow, reduces congestion, and enhances road safety through real-time analysis of traffic patterns.

AI in Human Resources: AI assists in talent acquisition, employee engagement, and workforce optimization through data analysis.

AI-based Financial Planning: AI algorithms analyze financial data to provide personalized investment advice, budgeting, and financial planning.

Predicting Equipment Failures: AI applications analyze data from machinery sensors to predict and prevent equipment failures in industrial settings.

Language Preservation: AI aids in preserving endangered languages by analyzing linguistic data, documenting, and generating language content.

The Dark Side: Pitfalls, Ethical Considerations, and Fears of AI

In the ever-evolving landscape of technology, Artificial Intelligence (AI) stands as a beacon of innovation. However, "The Dark Side: Pitfalls, Ethical Considerations, and Fears of AI," delves into the shadows that often shroud this transformative technology. Beyond ethical concerns, it addresses the pervasive fears that AI instills in people, contributing to a nuanced understanding of the apprehensions surrounding this powerful innovation.

Bias and Discrimination:

The mid-section of this chapter explores a fundamental fear associated with AI—the perpetuation of bias and discrimination. People are wary that AI systems, if not rigorously monitored, might inadvertently replicate and exacerbate societal prejudices. Instances of biased outcomes in areas like hiring, criminal justice, and facial recognition technologies fuel concerns about systemic inequalities being perpetuated by AI.

The fear that AI might amplify existing biases prompts discussions on the ethical responsibility of developers, researchers, and policymakers to ensure fairness in AI algorithms. Understanding these concerns is essential for crafting strategies that mitigate bias and discrimination in AI applications.

Privacy Invasion:

Another source of apprehension revolves around the invasion of privacy through AI-driven surveillance systems. The mid-section scrutinizes the fear that advanced data analytics and facial recognition technologies may encroach upon personal freedoms. The pervasiveness of surveillance, both in public spaces and private domains, raises alarms about the erosion of individual privacy.

Examining real-world scenarios where AI-powered systems have been deployed for surveillance underscores the need for stringent regulations and ethical guidelines to strike a balance between security and the right to personal privacy.

Job Displacement and Economic Disparity:

Fear of job displacement due to automation powered by AI is a prevalent concern among the workforce. The mid-section delves into the anxiety surrounding the potential loss of jobs as machines take on routine tasks. The fear is not only about unemployment but also the potential exacerbation of economic disparities.

This section emphasizes the need for proactive measures, including education and retraining programs, to equip the workforce for the evolving job market. Addressing these concerns is crucial for fostering a sense of security and resilience in the face of technological disruptions.

Lack of Accountability and Transparency:

The opacity of certain AI algorithms and decision-making processes gives rise to fears regarding accountability and transparency. The mid-section explores the anxiety stemming from the inability to comprehend how AI systems reach decisions, especially in critical domains like healthcare and criminal justice.

This fear underscores the importance of demanding transparency and explainability in AI systems, ensuring that users can trust and understand the technologies influencing their lives.

General Fears Surrounding AI:

In addition to these specific concerns, people harbor general fears about the unknown aspects of AI. The fear of losing control to autonomous systems, the fear of job markets being reshaped by AI, and the fear of AI systems surpassing human intelligence are overarching anxieties that contribute to apprehension.

Addressing these fears involves demystifying AI, fostering education and awareness, and actively involving the public in discussions surrounding AI development and deployment.

As we navigate the fears associated with AI, it becomes clear that addressing these concerns requires a holistic and collaborative approach. Understanding the fears of bias, privacy invasion, job displacement, lack of accountability, and general uncertainties is the first step toward responsible AI development.

This chapter serves as a bridge between the ethical considerations and the fears that permeate public discourse around AI. Recognizing and addressing these fears are integral to building trust and ensuring that AI is developed and utilized in ways that align with human values and societal well-being.

In the chapters that follow, the focus will shift to potential solutions, regulations, and ethical frameworks that can help mitigate these fears, fostering a more positive and inclusive narrative around the future of AI.

Fears of AI:

Loss of Control to Autonomous Systems:

One prevailing fear surrounding AI is the potential loss of control to autonomous systems. As AI technologies become more sophisticated, there's a growing apprehension that humans may relinquish control over decision-making processes to machines. The fear is not just about machines making decisions but about their ability to learn and adapt independently, potentially surpassing human understanding.

This fear taps into a broader concern about the ethical implications of granting autonomy to AI systems, especially in contexts where critical decisions impacting individuals or society are at stake. Striking a balance between leveraging the benefits of autonomous systems and maintaining human oversight becomes a crucial consideration in addressing this fear.

Impact on Job Markets:

The fear of AI reshaping job markets is multifaceted. Beyond the concern of job displacement due to automation, there's an anxiety about the transformation of entire industries and the types of skills that will be valued in the future job market. As AI assumes routine tasks, there's uncertainty about the nature of new job opportunities and the adaptability of the workforce to evolving job requirements.

This fear underscores the importance of comprehensive strategies for workforce development, including reskilling and upskilling initiatives. Proactively addressing the impact of AI on employment is essential for assuaging concerns and fostering a sense of security in the face of technological change.

AI Surpassing Human Intelligence:

A deep-seated fear revolves around the concept of AI surpassing human intelligence—a scenario often referred to as the technological singularity. The concern is not just about machines becoming smarter, but about the potential consequences of creating entities that outstrip human cognitive abilities.

This fear delves into the realms of science fiction, raising existential questions about the relationship between humans and AI. While current AI systems are far from achieving general intelligence comparable to humans, the fear prompts discussions about ethical guidelines and safeguards that should be in place as AI technologies advance.

Ethical Dilemmas and Decision-Making:

The fear of ethical dilemmas and biased decision-making by AI systems permeates discussions on responsible AI deployment. Concerns arise from the realization that AI algorithms, when trained on biased data or inadequately monitored, can perpetuate and even exacerbate societal prejudices.

This fear emphasizes the need for ongoing scrutiny and evaluation of AI systems to ensure fairness and ethical behavior. Implementing guidelines for ethical AI development, testing, and continuous monitoring becomes crucial in addressing this apprehension and building public trust.

Societal Impact and Inequality:

Beyond individual concerns, there's a broader fear about the societal impact of AI contributing to increased inequality. The fear is that AI technologies may be adopted more rapidly by certain industries or countries, leading to a technological divide. This fear extends beyond employment to encompass broader issues of access to technology, education, and economic opportunities.

Addressing this fear involves not only technological considerations but also the formulation of policies and initiatives that promote equitable access to and benefits from AI advancements. Striving for inclusivity and considering the broader societal implications of AI adoption are integral in mitigating this particular concern.

Understanding and addressing the fears associated with AI is a complex but necessary endeavor. While acknowledging the legitimate concerns, it is essential to approach these fears with a balanced perspective that considers the potential benefits of AI alongside its challenges.

In the subsequent chapters, the focus will shift towards exploring solutions, ethical frameworks, and regulatory measures that aim to alleviate these fears and ensure the responsible development and deployment of AI technologies. A nuanced and comprehensive approach is essential to foster a positive narrative around the future integration of AI into various aspects of human life.

Will A.I. It Take Over Humanity and Make Them Slaves?

The advent of Artificial Intelligence (AI) has sparked a cascade of awe and trepidation. Among the myriad questions and concerns, a haunting fear whispers through the corridors of our collective imagination: will AI take over humanity, reducing us to mere pawns in its grand design? This fear of AI enslaving humanity is rooted in both the possibilities and uncertainties that this transformative technology presents.

The Landscape of Fear:

Sci-Fi Nightmares Turned Real?

The fear of AI taking over humanity echoes the dystopian narratives spun by science fiction for decades. From "The Matrix" to "Blade Runner," these cautionary tales depict a future where machines rebel against their human creators, dominating and subjugating the very architects of their existence. While these scenarios belong to the realm of fiction, the fear lingers as AI evolves and permeates more aspects of our lives.

The Paradox of Autonomy:

Central to this fear is the notion of AI achieving a level of autonomy that surpasses human control. The paradox lies in our desire to create intelligent, self-learning systems while simultaneously fearing that these systems might surpass our ability to manage them. The fear extends beyond the physical realm, delving into the intricacies of decision-making, ethics, and the potential consequences of ceding control to autonomous entities.

Analyzing the Fear:

Technological Singularity:

At the heart of the fear lies the concept of technological singularity, a hypothetical point where AI reaches a level of intelligence surpassing that of humans. The concern is not just about AI matching human intellect but potentially exceeding it, leading to a cascade of rapid self-improvement cycles that could render human control obsolete.

This fear raises existential questions about the relationship between humans and machines. Will AI develop motivations, desires, or objectives that misalign with our values? The fear of losing control to a superintelligent entity is an existential dilemma that fuels debates on ethical AI development and regulation.

Ethical Dilemmas:

Another facet of the fear revolves around ethical considerations. The worry is not merely about AI becoming autonomous but about the decisions it might make when faced with complex moral dilemmas. The fear is rooted in the understanding that AI systems, driven by algorithms and data, may lack the nuanced ethical compass inherent in human decision-making.

Concerns about biases, discrimination, and unforeseen consequences in AI decision-making processes contribute to the broader fear of AI becoming an uncontrollable force with the potential to perpetuate societal injustices.

Grounding the Fear in Reality:

Current State of AI:

As of now, the fear of AI taking over humanity and making us slaves is more speculative than grounded in current realities. AI, in its current state, is a tool developed and controlled by humans. While advancements are swift, the level of autonomy and intelligence attributed to AI in fictional narratives is yet to materialize.

Current AI systems are designed for specific tasks and lack a holistic understanding of the world. They operate within defined parameters set by human programmers, and their actions are constrained by the limitations of their programming. The fear of an imminent AI uprising tends to overlook the significant challenges in achieving true autonomy and understanding.

The Role of Regulation and Ethics:

To assuage these fears, a crucial aspect lies in the implementation of robust regulations and ethical guidelines governing AI development. Governments, researchers, and industry leaders are increasingly recognizing the need for responsible AI practices. Initiatives promoting transparency, fairness, and accountability aim to ensure that AI aligns with human values and remains a tool for societal benefit rather than a force of subjugation.

Navigating the Path Forward:

The Call for Ethical AI:

Rather than succumbing to unfounded fears, the emphasis should be on fostering ethical AI development. Ethical guidelines can steer AI towards becoming a collaborative force, augmenting human capabilities while respecting our values and principles.

The integration of diverse perspectives in AI development, including ethicists, sociologists, and representatives from various communities, can contribute to creating AI systems that are not only intelligent but also aligned with human morals and societal well-being.

Public Awareness and Engagement:

Addressing the fear of AI enslaving humanity requires active public engagement and awareness. Understanding the current capabilities and limitations of AI, as well as the ongoing efforts to ensure responsible development, can empower individuals to participate in shaping the trajectory of AI.

Public discourse on AI should extend beyond fear to include discussions on the ethical implications, regulatory frameworks, and the collaborative efforts needed to ensure AI remains a tool that serves humanity rather than dominates it.

The fear of AI taking over humanity and turning us into slaves is a complex narrative woven from both rational concerns and speculative fiction. As AI continues to evolve, the emphasis should be on responsible development, ethical considerations, and collaborative frameworks that align with human values.

The path forward requires a collective commitment to shaping AI as a force for good. By dispelling unfounded fears, fostering awareness, and actively participating in the ethical discourse surrounding AI, humanity can guide this transformative technology towards a future where autonomy coexists with human values, rather than overriding them.

AI in Medicine: A Lifesaving Innovation

In the ever-evolving landscape of technological innovation, Artificial Intelligence (AI) emerges as a beacon of hope within the realm of medicine. Chapter 7, "AI in Medicine: A Lifesaving Innovation," delves into the transformative impact of AI in healthcare, exploring how intelligent algorithms and machine learning applications are revolutionizing diagnostics, treatment plans, and overall patient care.

As we embark on this exploration, it becomes evident that the marriage of AI and medicine holds immense potential to save lives, improve efficiency, and enhance medical outcomes. This chapter unfolds the intricate tapestry of AI applications in healthcare, spotlighting real-life examples, including its crucial role during the COVID-19 pandemic.

AI in Diagnostics: Precision Unleashed

The mid-section of this chapter delves into the profound impact of AI on diagnostics, where precision and speed are paramount. AI algorithms, fueled by vast datasets and intricate learning models, can analyze medical images with an unprecedented level of accuracy. From detecting subtle abnormalities in radiological scans to identifying early signs of diseases, AI-powered diagnostics have proven to be a game-changer.

Real-life Example: COVID-19 Detection

During the COVID-19 pandemic, AI played a pivotal role in expediting the diagnosis of the virus. Chest X-rays and CT scans, analyzed by AI algorithms, aided healthcare professionals in swiftly identifying patterns indicative of COVID-19 pneumonia. This not only facilitated quicker patient triage but also alleviated the burden on healthcare systems inundated with cases, showcasing AI's ability to enhance diagnostic efficiency during critical times.

Treatment Personalization: Tailoring Healthcare to Individuals

The chapter continues by exploring how AI is transforming treatment plans, ushering in an era of personalized medicine. By analyzing patient data, genetic information, and treatment outcomes, AI can identify optimal therapeutic approaches tailored to an individual's unique characteristics. This not only maximizes treatment efficacy but also minimizes side effects, marking a paradigm shift in how healthcare is delivered.

Real-life Example: Genomic Medicine

In the realm of genomic medicine, AI has been instrumental in decoding the complexities of genetic data. AI algorithms analyze vast genomic datasets to identify genetic markers associated with diseases, allowing for personalized treatment strategies. This breakthrough is exemplified in cancer care, where AI assists in matching patients with targeted therapies based on their genetic profiles, leading to more effective and less invasive treatments.

AI-enhanced Clinical Decision Support Systems

Moving forward, the chapter explores the integration of AI into clinical decision support systems. These intelligent tools assist healthcare professionals by providing data-driven insights, evidence-based recommendations, and predictive analytics. By leveraging AI, clinicians can make informed decisions, anticipate patient needs, and optimize care delivery.

Real-life Example: Predictive Analytics in ICU

In intensive care units (ICUs), AI-driven predictive analytics have been employed to foresee deteriorations in patients' conditions. By analyzing real-time physiological data, AI algorithms can identify subtle changes that may precede critical events, enabling proactive interventions. This not only improves patient outcomes but also enhances resource utilization in healthcare settings, showcasing the potential of AI in optimizing clinical decision-making.

The Role of AI in Telemedicine

As the chapter unfolds, the spotlight shifts to the role of AI in telemedicine—a facet that gained prominence, especially during the COVID-19 pandemic. AI-driven telehealth solutions have facilitated remote consultations, diagnostic assessments, and continuous monitoring. This has not only increased accessibility to healthcare services but also minimized the risk of viral transmission.

Remote Patient Monitoring during COVID-19

During the peak of the COVID-19 pandemic, AI-powered remote patient monitoring played a crucial role in tracking patients' vital signs and symptoms from their homes. Wearable devices and smartphone applications, integrated with AI algorithms, enabled healthcare providers to remotely assess patients' conditions, intervening promptly when necessary. This innovative use of AI in telemedicine demonstrated its capacity to extend medical care beyond physical boundaries, ensuring continuous monitoring and timely interventions.

As we conclude our exploration of AI in medicine, it becomes evident that this innovative fusion is reshaping the healthcare landscape. From precision diagnostics to personalized treatment plans, AI is ushering in a new era of lifesaving innovations. Real-life examples, particularly those from the challenges posed by the COVID-19 pandemic, underscore the tangible benefits of AI in enhancing healthcare delivery.

The collaborative synergy between human expertise and AI capabilities is forging a path toward more effective, efficient, and patient-centric healthcare. The potential for AI to save lives, optimize treatments, and navigate the complexities of modern medicine is not a distant dream but a tangible reality unfolding in clinics and hospitals worldwide.

As we look to the future, the continued integration of AI in medicine holds the promise of further breakthroughs, making healthcare not only more technologically advanced but also more compassionate and tailored to the unique needs of each individual. In the subsequent chapters, we will continue to explore the multifaceted landscape of AI applications, unraveling its potential to bring about positive transformations in various domains of human life.

Artificial Intelligence (AI) has played a crucial role in saving lives in environments where human presence is challenging or impossible due to natural disasters, extreme conditions, or extraterrestrial locations. Here are two scenarios where AI has been instrumental in mitigating risks and aiding in life-saving efforts:

Tremendous help of AI in Disaster Response

Landslide Sites

The Challenge:

Landslides pose a significant threat to human life, often occurring in remote or challenging terrains. Accessing landslide sites quickly and efficiently is critical for search and rescue operations, but the unpredictable nature of landslides and the risk of further instability make it perilous for human responders.

AI Applications:

1. **Satellite Imaging and Remote Sensing:** AI algorithms process satellite imagery and remote sensing data to identify potential landslide sites and assess the extent of the damage. Machine learning models can analyze historical data, topographical features,

and weather conditions to predict areas prone to landslides, enabling proactive measures.

2.   **Drones for Rapid Assessment:** AI-powered drones equipped with high-resolution cameras and sensors can navigate difficult terrain and capture real-time images of landslide-affected areas. AI image analysis helps identify survivors, assess the severity of the situation, and guide rescue teams with actionable insights.

3.   **Predictive Analytics for Early Warning Systems:** AI-based predictive models analyze various parameters, including rainfall patterns, soil moisture levels, and geological data, to forecast potential landslide events. Early warning systems powered by AI can alert communities and authorities, providing valuable time for evacuation and preparation.

Real-world Example:

In recent landslide events, AI technologies have been deployed to process satellite imagery and aerial data swiftly. These AI-driven analyses helped emergency responders identify areas with the highest risk and allocate resources effectively, minimizing response time and improving the chances of survival for those affected.

Space Exploration: Extraterrestrial Environments

The Challenge:

Exploring outer space presents numerous challenges due to extreme conditions, lack of a habitable atmosphere, and vast distances. Sending humans into such environments poses substantial risks to life, making it imperative to rely on AI for space exploration.

AI Applications

1.   **Autonomous Robotics:** AI-powered robots and rovers are deployed in space missions to explore planetary surfaces. These

machines can navigate challenging terrains, collect samples, and perform experiments autonomously. AI algorithms enable these robots to adapt to unforeseen obstacles and make decisions without direct human intervention.

2.   **Space Probes and Telescopes:** AI enhances the capabilities of space probes and telescopes by autonomously selecting targets for observation, adjusting instruments in response to changing conditions, and analyzing vast amounts of astronomical data. This enables astronomers to make groundbreaking discoveries without the limitations of human-operated systems.

3.   **Life Support Systems:** In space habitats, AI is utilized in life support systems to monitor environmental conditions, manage oxygen levels, and regulate temperature. These systems ensure the well-being of astronauts in the absence of a hospitable atmosphere.

Real-world Example:

During Mars exploration missions, AI played a pivotal role in the operation of rovers like Curiosity. These rovers autonomously navigated the Martian terrain, conducted scientific experiments, and transmitted data back to Earth. The use of AI in space exploration has expanded our understanding of celestial bodies and laid the groundwork for future manned missions.

AI's ability to operate in inhospitable environments, process vast amounts of data, and make decisions in real-time positions it as a valuable asset in scenarios where human presence is limited or too risky. Whether responding to natural disasters on Earth or exploring the vastness of space, AI continues to contribute to life-saving efforts and expand the boundaries of what is achievable in challenging environments.

A.I Saving Human Lives

50 additional real-world examples where AI has played a crucial role in saving human lives:

Early Cancer Detection:

AI algorithms analyze medical images to detect early signs of cancer, improving prognosis and treatment outcomes.

Drug Discovery:

AI accelerates drug discovery processes, identifying potential treatments for various diseases more efficiently.

Fall Detection for Elderly:

AI-powered systems monitor the movements of elderly individuals, detecting falls and triggering immediate assistance.

Automated External Defibrillators (AEDs):

AI enhances AEDs, providing real-time guidance for bystanders during cardiac emergencies.

Firefighting Drones:

Drones equipped with AI algorithms help firefighters assess and combat wildfires, minimizing risks to human responders.

Trauma Triage in Emergency Rooms:

AI aids in prioritizing and triaging patients in emergency rooms based on the severity of their conditions.

Autonomous Vehicles:

AI-driven autonomous vehicles contribute to reducing road accidents by improving driving safety.

Opioid Overdose Prediction:

AI models analyze patient data to predict and prevent opioid overdoses in healthcare settings.

Air Quality Monitoring:

AI monitors air quality in real-time, alerting communities to potential health hazards and pollution levels.

Disease Outbreak Prediction:

AI analyzes data patterns to predict and monitor disease outbreaks, aiding in early containment efforts.

Suicide Prevention Chatbots:

AI-powered chatbots provide support and intervention for individuals at risk of suicide.

Automated CPR Guidance:

AI guides individuals performing CPR, ensuring proper chest compressions during cardiac emergencies.

Hospital Resource Optimization:

AI optimizes hospital resources, ensuring efficient allocation of beds, staff, and medical supplies.

Automated Seizure Detection:

AI algorithms analyze EEG data to detect seizures in epilepsy patients, enabling timely interventions.

Pandemic Response Planning:

AI assists in planning and executing effective responses during global pandemics, as seen in COVID-19.

Asthma Management:

AI-powered inhalers monitor usage patterns and provide personalized insights for asthma management.

Predictive Policing:

AI helps law enforcement predict and prevent crimes by analyzing historical data and patterns.

Robotic Surgery:

AI-assisted robotic surgery enhances precision and reduces risks in complex medical procedures.

Water Quality Monitoring:

AI monitors water quality in real-time, detecting contaminants and ensuring safe drinking water.

Automated Diabetic Retinopathy Screening:

AI analyzes retinal images to detect diabetic retinopathy, preventing vision loss in diabetic patients.

Smart Prosthetics:

AI enhances the functionality of prosthetic limbs, adapting to users' movements and providing more natural control.

Airplane Crash Prediction:

AI analyzes flight data to predict potential safety issues and contribute to proactive maintenance.

Antibiotic Resistance Monitoring:

AI monitors and predicts antibiotic resistance patterns, guiding healthcare professionals in choosing effective treatments.

Food Safety Inspections:

AI automates food safety inspections, identifying potential hazards and ensuring compliance with regulations.

Remote Monitoring for Chronic Diseases:

AI facilitates remote monitoring of patients with chronic diseases, enabling timely interventions and reducing hospital visits.

Automated Medication Dispensing:

AI-driven medication dispensing systems reduce errors and ensure accurate medication administration.

Predictive Analytics for Sepsis:

AI predicts the onset of sepsis by analyzing patient data, allowing for early intervention and treatment.

Mental Health Apps:

AI-powered mental health apps provide personalized support, monitoring users' emotional well-being and offering coping strategies.

Humanitarian Aid Distribution:

AI optimizes the distribution of humanitarian aid in crisis situations, ensuring efficient resource allocation.

Wildlife Conservation:

AI assists in wildlife conservation efforts by monitoring animal populations, identifying endangered species, and detecting poaching activities.

Automated Fire Detection:

AI analyzes satellite imagery and sensors to detect wildfires in their early stages, enabling rapid response.

Speech and Language Disorders Diagnosis:

AI aids in diagnosing speech and language disorders in children, facilitating early intervention and therapy.

Smart Hearing Aids:

AI-driven hearing aids adapt to different environments, enhancing the auditory experience for users.

Predictive Analytics for Heart Conditions:

AI analyzes heart rate and other vital signs to predict and prevent heart conditions.

Humanitarian Drone Delivery:

Drones equipped with AI navigate challenging terrains to deliver medical supplies and aid in humanitarian missions.

Automated Blood Pressure Monitoring:

AI-powered devices monitor blood pressure trends, alerting users and healthcare professionals to potential issues.

Monitoring Sleep Disorders:

AI analyzes sleep patterns and data from wearables to identify and manage sleep disorders.

Emergency Response Coordination:

AI assists in coordinating emergency responses, optimizing the deployment of resources during disasters.

Visual Impairment Assistance:

AI-powered devices assist individuals with visual impairments by providing real-time object recognition and navigation guidance.

Disease Surveillance in Animals:

AI monitors animal health, helping prevent the spread of diseases from animals to humans.

Automated Skin Cancer Detection:

AI analyzes images of skin lesions to detect early signs of skin cancer, aiding in timely diagnosis.

Personalized Vaccination Plans:

Automated Blood Pressure Monitoring:

AI-powered devices monitor blood pressure trends, alerting users and healthcare professionals to potential issues.

Monitoring Sleep Disorders:

AI analyzes sleep patterns and data from wearables to identify and manage sleep disorders.

Emergency Response Coordination:

AI assists in coordinating emergency responses, optimizing the deployment of resources during disasters.

Visual Impairment Assistance:

AI-powered devices assist individuals with visual impairments by providing real-time object recognition and navigation guidance.

Disease Surveillance in Animals:

AI monitors animal health, helping prevent the spread of diseases from animals to humans.

Automated Skin Cancer Detection:

AI analyzes images of skin lesions to detect early signs of skin cancer, aiding in timely diagnosis.

Personalized Vaccination Plans:

AI assists in developing personalized vaccination plans, optimizing vaccine schedules for individuals.

Drowning Detection Systems:

AI-powered surveillance systems can detect drowning incidents in swimming pools, beaches, and other water bodies.

Automated Language Translation for Emergency Communication:

AI aids in translating languages in real-time during emergency situations, facilitating communication with diverse populations.

Sleep Apnea Monitoring:

AI analyzes sleep patterns and respiratory data to monitor and manage sleep apnea.

Remote Monitoring of Infants in Neonatal Intensive Care Units (NICU):

AI assists in monitoring the vital signs of premature infants in NICUs, providing early alerts to medical staff.

Automated Cholesterol Level Monitoring:

AI-driven devices monitor cholesterol levels, offering timely insights for cardiovascular health.

Smart Contact Lenses for Diabetes Management:

AI-integrated contact lenses monitor glucose levels in tears, aiding in diabetes management.

Automated Allergy Management:

AI helps individuals manage allergies by analyzing environmental data and providing personalized recommendations.

Earthquake Early Warning Systems:

AI analyzes seismic data to predict and provide early warnings for earthquakes, allowing for preparedness and evacuation.

These examples underscore the diverse and impactful ways in which AI is contributing to saving lives across various domains and challenging environments. From healthcare and disaster response to wildlife conservation and space exploration, AI continues to be a transformative force for the betterment of humanity.

Environmental Monitoring and Disaster Response

Hurricane Tracking and Prediction:

AI analyzes weather patterns to predict the paths and intensities of hurricanes, aiding in evacuation planning.

Earthquake Damage Assessment:

AI processes satellite imagery to assess the extent of damage caused by earthquakes, guiding relief efforts.

Wildfire Prediction and Prevention:

AI models analyze various factors, including weather conditions and vegetation, to predict and prevent wildfires.

Tsunami Early Warning Systems:

AI monitors seismic activities and oceanic conditions to provide early warnings for potential tsunamis.

Flood Monitoring and Mitigation:

AI-powered sensors and satellite data monitor water levels, predicting and mitigating the impact of floods.

Extreme Temperature Event Prediction:

AI analyzes historical climate data to predict extreme temperature events, helping communities prepare.

Volcanic Eruption Monitoring:

AI processes data from ground-based and satellite sensors to monitor volcanic activity and issue warnings.

Avalanche Risk Assessment:

AI algorithms analyze terrain and weather conditions to assess and predict avalanche risks in mountainous regions.

Drought Prediction and Agriculture Support:

AI predicts drought conditions, aiding farmers in optimizing water usage and crop planning.

Crisis Mapping for Emergency Response:

AI processes real-time data to create dynamic crisis maps, guiding emergency responders during disasters.

Space Exploration and Extraterrestrial Research

Autonomous Mars Rovers:

AI enables autonomous navigation and decision-making for Mars rovers, exploring the Martian surface.

Exoplanet Discovery:

AI algorithms analyze astronomical data to identify potential exoplanets in distant star systems.

Space Debris Tracking:

AI tracks and predicts the movement of space debris, preventing collisions with satellites and spacecraft.

Autonomous Space Probes:

AI assists space probes in autonomously navigating through space, collecting data on celestial bodies.

Remote Sensing for Lunar Exploration:

AI-enhanced remote sensing technologies aid in lunar exploration, mapping and analyzing lunar terrain.

Space Weather Prediction:

AI models analyze solar and cosmic activity to predict space weather, protecting satellites and astronauts.

Extraterrestrial Life Search:

AI processes data from telescopes and satellites in the search for potential signs of extraterrestrial life.

Autonomous Satellites for Earth Observation:

AI-driven satellites capture and analyze Earth's surface changes, supporting environmental monitoring.

Asteroid Detection and Deflection:

AI assists in the detection of potentially hazardous asteroids and proposes deflection strategies.

Robotic Repair and Maintenance in Space:

AI-driven robots conduct repairs and maintenance on satellites and space stations in orbit.

Healthcare and Medical Innovation

Telemedicine in Remote Areas:

AI facilitates telemedicine, connecting patients in remote areas with healthcare professionals.

AI-Powered Prosthetics:

AI enhances the functionality of prosthetic limbs, adapting to users' movements in real-time.

Remote Robotic Surgery:

AI assists surgeons in conducting remote surgeries using robotic systems, overcoming geographical barriers.

Drug Repurposing for Epidemics:

AI accelerates the identification of existing drugs that could be repurposed for new epidemics.

AI-Enhanced Gene Editing:

AI aids in designing precise gene-editing strategies, advancing research in genetic therapies.

Automated Medical Imaging Analysis:

AI analyzes medical images, detecting abnormalities in X-rays, MRIs, and other diagnostic scans.

AI in Organ Transplant Matching:

AI optimizes the matching process for organ transplants, improving success rates and reducing waiting times.

Remote Patient Monitoring for Chronic Diseases:

AI enables remote monitoring of patients with chronic diseases, ensuring timely interventions.

Drug Dosage Optimization:

AI assists in determining optimal drug dosages for individual patients, minimizing side effects.

AI in Mental Health Diagnostics:

AI models analyze speech patterns and behavioral data for early detection of mental health conditions.

Humanitarian Aid and Crisis Response

Refugee Aid and Resource Allocation:

AI aids humanitarian organizations in allocating resources efficiently during refugee crises.

Automated Language Translation in Crisis Zones:

AI-powered translation services assist communication in multilingual crisis zones.

Disease Tracking during Humanitarian Crises:

AI analyzes data to track and predict disease outbreaks in areas affected by humanitarian crises.

Blockchain for Humanitarian Aid Distribution:

AI-driven blockchain systems enhance transparency and efficiency in distributing humanitarian aid.

Automated Rescue Drones:

AI-powered drones assist in search and rescue operations during natural disasters and emergencies.

Precision Humanitarian Mapping:

AI processes satellite imagery for detailed mapping, aiding in targeted humanitarian interventions.

Water Purification Optimization:

AI optimizes water purification processes in crisis-stricken areas, ensuring access to clean water.

Automated Refugee Status Determination:

AI assists in processing and determining refugee status, expediting legal processes.

AI in Epidemic Preparedness:

AI models predict and prepare for potential epidemics in vulnerable regions, guiding proactive measures.

Food Security Monitoring:

AI monitors agricultural conditions and predicts food shortages, supporting humanitarian efforts.

Safety and Security Applications

Anti-Poaching Surveillance:

AI-powered cameras and drones monitors continue on safety and security applications

Anti-Poaching Surveillance:

AI-powered cameras and drones monitor wildlife reserves, detecting and alerting authorities to potential poaching activities.

AI-Powered Cyber security:

AI algorithms analyze network behavior to detect and prevent cyber threats, safeguarding digital infrastructure.

Smart Surveillance for Public Safety:

AI enhances surveillance systems in public spaces, identifying suspicious behavior and enhancing overall safety.

Autonomous Border Security:

AI-driven autonomous systems monitor and secure borders, detecting unauthorized border crossings.

AI in Emergency Services Dispatch:

AI assists emergency services in analyzing incoming calls and dispatching resources efficiently during crises.

Facial Recognition for Law Enforcement:

AI-powered facial recognition technologies aid law enforcement agencies in identifying and apprehending suspects.

Predictive Policing for Crime Prevention:

AI models analyze historical crime data to predict and prevent criminal activities in specific areas.

Smart Traffic Management:

AI optimizes traffic flow and reduces congestion, improving road safety and emergency response times.

AI in Disaster Recovery Planning:

AI aids in disaster recovery planning by analyzing data to predict and mitigate long-term impacts.

Personal Safety Wearables:

AI-driven wearables, such as smart bracelets, provide real-time safety alerts and location tracking for individuals in distress.

These safety and security applications highlight the diverse ways in which AI technology is contributing to the protection and well-being of individuals and communities in challenging and extreme conditions. From disaster response to public safety and beyond, AI continues to play a pivotal role in creating safer environments and mitigating risks.

Transforming Industries - AI's Impact on Business

In the ever-evolving landscape of technology, Artificial Intelligence (AI) stands at the forefront of transformative change, reshaping the very foundations of industries across the globe. Chapter 8, "Transforming Industries: AI's Impact on Business," embarks on a journey to unravel the profound influence AI exerts on diverse sectors, redefining the way businesses operate, strategize, and innovate.

As we delve into this exploration, it becomes evident that AI is not merely a technological tool; it is a catalyst for a new era of efficiency, innovation, and competitiveness. This chapter navigates through the dynamic interplay of AI and various industries, shedding light on how businesses leverage intelligent algorithms, data analytics, and automation to gain a strategic edge in an increasingly digital world.

1. AI in Operations and Efficiency:

The transformative impact of AI on business operations is undeniable. Intelligent automation streamlines routine tasks, enhancing efficiency and freeing up human resources for more complex endeavors. From supply chain optimization to logistics management, AI algorithms analyze vast datasets in real-time, enabling businesses to make data-driven decisions, minimize costs, and respond swiftly to market dynamics.

2. Enhancing Customer Experiences:

AI-driven personalization has become a cornerstone of customer experiences. Through advanced analytics and machine learning, businesses tailor their offerings to individual preferences, delivering targeted content, recommendations, and services. Virtual assistants and chatbots powered by AI provide seamless interactions, resolving queries, and enhancing customer satisfaction. The mid section unfolds how AI is not only meeting but exceeding customer expectations, fostering loyalty and trust.

3. Innovating Product Development:

The intersection of AI and product development is marked by unprecedented innovation. From ideation to design and prototyping, AI accelerates the creative process, identifying trends and predicting consumer demands. In fields like pharmaceuticals, AI expedites drug discovery, reducing timeframes for research and development. The mid section of this chapter unravels the ways in which AI is not just a tool but a driving force behind novel products and services.

4. Strategic Decision-Making with AI:

In the boardrooms of the modern business landscape, AI has become an indispensable ally in strategic decision-making. Advanced analytics and predictive modeling enable executives to make informed choices, foresee market trends, and navigate uncertainties. The mid section delves into real-world examples where AI empowers businesses to anticipate challenges, identify opportunities, and chart a course towards sustainable growth.

5. AI in Marketing and Advertising:

The marketing landscape has undergone a paradigm shift with the infusion of AI. Targeted advertising, dynamic pricing, and personalized campaigns are no longer aspirations but realities. AI analyzes consumer behavior, optimizing marketing strategies and ensuring a more significant return on investment. This section explores how businesses harness the power of AI to create compelling narratives, engage audiences, and stay ahead in the competitive market.

6. Cybersecurity and Risk Mitigation:

As businesses traverse the digital realm, the need for robust cybersecurity measures has never been more critical. AI-powered cybersecurity solutions go beyond traditional approaches, identifying and preempting potential threats in real-time. The mid section elucidates how AI is instrumental in safeguarding sensitive data, fortifying digital infrastructures, and mitigating risks posed by an evolving threat landscape.

7. AI and Workforce Transformation:

The integration of AI into business models necessitates a reevaluation of workforce dynamics. The mid section explores how AI augments human capabilities, creating a symbiotic relationship between technology and talent. Upskilling and reskilling initiatives, coupled with AI-driven collaboration, redefine traditional job roles and pave the way for a more agile, adaptable workforce.

8. Ethical Considerations in AI Implementation:

As AI becomes ubiquitous in business operations, ethical considerations come to the forefront. Bias in algorithms, data privacy concerns, and the responsible use of AI demand careful scrutiny. This section navigates the ethical landscape, discussing frameworks and practices that businesses adopt to ensure the responsible deployment of AI technologies.

As we draw the curtain on this exploration of AI's impact on business, it becomes evident that we are witnessing a seismic shift in the way industries operate and innovate. AI has transcended the realm of a technological tool to become a strategic enabler, a catalyst for reinvention and resilience in the face of an ever-changing business landscape.

The transformation of industries through AI is not a one-size-fits-all phenomenon; it is a nuanced journey where businesses must navigate challenges, embrace opportunities, and continually adapt to the evolving technological tapestry. The chapter's conclusion underscores the imperative for businesses to adopt a forward-thinking mindset, fostering a culture of innovation, collaboration, and ethical responsibility in the era of AI.

As industries continue to evolve, propelled by the relentless march of technology, businesses that strategically harness the power of AI will emerge as leaders, charting new territories and redefining the future of commerce. In the subsequent chapters, we will unravel more facets of AI's impact, delving into specific industries, emerging trends, and the overarching implications for the global business ecosystem.

The Human Touch – A.I Way

Interactions with AI in Society, Solving Fundamental Problems Like Poverty

As Artificial Intelligence (AI) continues to weave its way into the fabric of society, its potential to address longstanding societal issues takes center stage. "The Human Touch: Interactions with AI in Society, Solving Fundamental Problems Like Poverty," embarks on a journey to explore how AI, coupled with the human touch, can be a catalyst for addressing age-old challenges such as poverty.

The chapter delves into the transformative possibilities of AI-human collaborations, emphasizing the importance of ethical deployment and human-centric approaches. It seeks to unfold a narrative where technology becomes an ally in the pursuit of creating a more equitable and inclusive society.

1. AI for Poverty Alleviation:

The mid section opens with a profound exploration of how AI, when strategically applied, can be a formidable force in the fight against poverty. Through data analytics, predictive modeling, and targeted interventions, AI empowers policymakers and organizations to design and implement effective poverty alleviation strategies. Real-world examples illuminate the transformative impact of AI in identifying vulnerable populations, optimizing resource allocation, and fostering sustainable development.

2. AI in Education: Bridging the Opportunity Gap:

Education emerges as a linchpin in breaking the cycle of poverty. The chapter unfolds how AI technologies enhance educational opportunities, offering personalized learning experiences and bridging the gap for disadvantaged communities. Adaptive learning platforms, intelligent tutoring systems, and AI-driven educational content become pivotal tools in fostering knowledge and skills that empower individuals to transcend socio-economic barriers.

3. AI-Enabled Healthcare for All:

The intersection of AI and healthcare takes center stage in this section, illustrating how advanced technologies can contribute to universal healthcare and poverty reduction. Telemedicine, AI diagnostics, and health monitoring systems are explored as tools that extend healthcare access to remote and underserved populations. The mid section articulates a vision where AI contributes to preventive care, early detection, and affordable medical solutions, laying the foundation for a healthier society.

4. AI for Financial Inclusion:

Economic empowerment is essential in the fight against poverty. Here, the chapter uncovers how AI-driven financial technologies foster financial inclusion, providing access to banking and credit services for individuals traditionally excluded from the financial system. Through innovations like mobile banking, AI-powered credit scoring, and microfinance platforms, the mid section outlines how technology can be a catalyst for economic independence and upward mobility.

5. Social Impact Entrepreneurship with AI:

The chapter navigates through the realm of social impact entrepreneurship, showcasing how AI can be harnessed to drive sustainable business models that prioritize social good. From AI-powered social enterprises to innovative solutions addressing local challenges, the mid section highlights how entrepreneurship, infused with a human touch, can create lasting positive change in communities grappling with poverty.

6. AI and Community Empowerment:

The mid section extends its focus to community-driven initiatives empowered by AI. Collaborative platforms, citizen-centric AI applications, and participatory decision-making processes are explored as tools that amplify the voices of marginalized communities. The chapter illuminates instances where AI becomes an enabler for grassroots movements, fostering community empowerment and resilience against the effects of poverty.

7. Ethical Considerations in AI-driven Social Solutions:

The ethical dimension of deploying AI for societal challenges takes center stage. This section delves into the importance of ethical frameworks, transparency, and community engagement in ensuring that AI solutions uphold human dignity, diversity, and inclusivity. It navigates through potential pitfalls, emphasizing the need for responsible AI practices that align with societal values.

As we draw the chapter to a close, the symbiotic relationship between AI and the human touch becomes a central theme. The transformative potential of AI in addressing fundamental issues like poverty is underscored, but with a crucial caveat—the importance of preserving human values, empathy, and ethical considerations throughout the journey.

In conclusion, this chapter envisions a future where AI-human interactions transcend technological advancements and encompass a deeper understanding of societal needs. The chapter advocates for collaborative efforts where AI is not viewed as a standalone solution but as a tool that amplifies human capabilities, enriches human experiences, and contributes to a more equitable and compassionate society.

The journey towards solving age-old problems requires not only technological prowess but a profound acknowledgment of the human condition. As we step into subsequent chapters, the exploration will continue, unveiling more dimensions where AI, guided by a human touch, becomes a force for positive societal transformation. The narrative unfolds, inviting stakeholders from diverse fields to actively engage in shaping a future where AI contributes to a world that leaves no one behind.

Bridging the Gap: Addressing the Persistent Struggle for Fundamental Rights

In an era marked by technological advancements, it is disheartening to witness the persisting challenges in fulfilling fundamental rights, especially regarding the provision of basic needs to impoverished populations worldwide. The stark disparity between the rich and the poor persists, raising critical questions about the failure of affluent individuals and nations to address this humanitarian crisis. In exploring this issue, it becomes evident that Artificial Intelligence (AI) holds the potential to revolutionize the approach to poverty alleviation and bridge the gap in fulfilling fundamental rights more efficiently than traditional methods.

The Global Struggle for Fundamental Rights

Despite numerous efforts and initiatives, a significant portion of the global population continues to grapple with the deprivation of fundamental rights. Access to basic needs such as food, clean water, healthcare, and education remains a distant dream for many, particularly in developing countries. The reasons behind this persistent struggle are multifaceted, encompassing economic, political, and social factors.

1. Economic Inequality:

Economic inequality stands as a major barrier to fulfilling fundamental rights. The concentration of wealth in the hands of a few exacerbates the disparities in access to resources and opportunities. The rich-poor divide widens as economic systems favor the affluent, leaving marginalized communities in a perpetual state of disadvantage.

2. Insufficient Social Welfare:

Inadequate social welfare systems contribute to the ongoing struggle. Many nations lack robust mechanisms to provide essential services and support to those in need. This absence of a safety net leaves vulnerable populations exposed to the harsh realities of poverty, hindering their ability to access education, healthcare, and other fundamental rights.

3. Political Instability and Corruption:

Political instability and corruption in various regions hinder the efficient allocation of resources for poverty alleviation. In some cases, resources intended for social welfare programs may be diverted or mismanaged, further exacerbating the challenges faced by the impoverished.

4. Lack of Education:

The lack of education perpetuates the cycle of poverty. Without access to quality education, individuals struggle to break free from the constraints of their circumstances, limiting their opportunities for economic and social advancement.

The Role of the Affluent in Addressing Fundamental Needs

The responsibility of addressing these challenges does not rest solely on the shoulders of governments and international organizations. Affluent individuals, including billionaires and successful entrepreneurs, bear a moral obligation to contribute meaningfully to society. However, there are notable shortcomings in their efforts to provide fundamental necessities to the poor.

1. Philanthropy Gaps:

While philanthropy has been a cornerstone of efforts to address social issues, there exist gaps in the distribution and impact of charitable endeavors. The lack of coordination, transparency, and strategic planning often results in inefficiencies, limiting the transformative potential of philanthropic initiatives.

2. Short-Term Solutions:

Many philanthropic efforts focus on short-term solutions rather than addressing the root causes of poverty. Temporary relief measures, while crucial in emergencies, may not lead to sustainable improvements in the long run.

3. Limited Scope:

The efforts of affluent individuals are often limited in scope, addressing specific issues or regions. A more comprehensive approach is needed to tackle the interconnected web of challenges that contribute to the persistence of poverty globally.

AI in Transforming Poverty Alleviation

As the world grapples with the limitations of traditional approaches, the integration of AI emerges as a promising solution to expedite poverty alleviation and fulfill fundamental rights. Here's how AI can play a pivotal role:

1. Data-Driven Decision-Making:

AI's capacity to analyze vast datasets in real-time enables informed decision-making. By leveraging data analytics, governments and organizations can identify areas of greatest need, allocate resources efficiently, and tailor interventions to address specific challenges faced by impoverished communities.

2. Predictive Modeling for Targeted Interventions:

AI's predictive modeling capabilities allow for the anticipation of future challenges. Whether it be anticipating food shortages, disease outbreaks, or educational needs, AI can help implement preemptive measures, ensuring a more proactive and effective response.

3. Smart Resource Allocation:

The optimization of resource allocation is a critical aspect of poverty alleviation. AI algorithms can analyze socio-economic indicators, demographic data, and geographical factors to recommend optimal resource distribution, minimizing waste and maximizing impact.

4. Personalized Education Solutions:

AI-powered educational tools offer personalized learning experiences, catering to individual needs and learning styles. This can significantly contribute to breaking the cycle of poverty by providing quality education that is accessible and tailored to the unique challenges faced by learners.

5. Job Creation and Economic Empowerment:

AI's role in job creation and economic empowerment cannot be overstated. Automation, when implemented responsibly, can free up human resources for more meaningful and higher-skilled tasks. Additionally, AI can support the growth of small businesses, fostering economic independence in impoverished communities.

6. Enhanced Philanthropic Impact:

AI can amplify the impact of philanthropy by providing data-driven insights into the most effective interventions. Strategic philanthropy, guided by AI analytics, can lead to more substantial and sustainable outcomes in poverty alleviation efforts.

7. Monitoring and Accountability:

AI-driven monitoring systems enhance accountability in poverty alleviation programs. Real-time tracking of resources, project outcomes, and social impact metrics ensures transparency and allows for continuous improvement in strategies.

The failure to fulfill fundamental rights and provide basic needs to impoverished populations is a complex challenge that demands innovative solutions. While traditional efforts have made strides, the integration of AI offers a paradigm shift in the approach to poverty alleviation. By leveraging the power of data, predictive analytics, and intelligent decision-making, AI has the potential to expedite progress and bring about transformative changes that lead to a more equitable and just world. The responsibility lies not only with governments and organizations but also with affluent individuals to embrace AI as a tool for positive social change. The path forward involves a collective commitment to harnessing technology responsibly and ensuring that AI becomes a force for good, ultimately realizing the vision of a world where fundamental rights are fulfilled for all.

A.I in Entertainment - Gaming to Creativity

In the ever-evolving landscape of technology, Artificial Intelligence (AI) has emerged as a transformative force in the realm of entertainment. From redefining gaming experiences to fostering creativity in content creation, AI's influence is reshaping how we engage with and consume entertainment. "Artificial Intelligence in Entertainment - From Gaming to Creativity," embarks on a journey to explore the multifaceted impact of AI in the entertainment industry.

This chapter delves into the intersection of AI and entertainment, highlighting the ways in which intelligent algorithms, machine learning, and creative applications are revolutionizing the way we play, watch, and interact with diverse forms of entertainment.

1. AI in Gaming: Elevating Player Experiences:

The mid section opens with an exploration of how AI is redefining the gaming landscape. From character behavior to dynamic storylines and personalized gaming experiences, AI algorithms are enhancing immersion and engagement. The section delves into the world of procedural content generation, where AI generates game content in real-time, creating limitless possibilities for gamers.

2. Virtual Characters and Conversational AI:

AI is playing a pivotal role in shaping virtual characters that exhibit human-like behaviors and respond intelligently to player actions. Conversational AI is explored as a tool for creating realistic dialogue, enabling more immersive narratives and enhancing the social aspect of gaming. This section unveils how AI is blurring the lines between the virtual and real worlds in gaming environments.

3. AI-Generated Music and Soundscapes:

The chapter transitions to the realm of sound and music in entertainment. AI's ability to analyze patterns and generate music that resonates with different moods and settings is unravelled. AI-generated soundscapes are explored for their role in creating ambient and dynamic audio environments, enriching the overall sensory experience in various entertainment mediums.

4. AI in Film and TV: Revolutionizing Content Creation:

AI's impact on the film and television industry takes center stage as the mid section unfolds. From scriptwriting assistance to virtual pre-visualization and post-production enhancements, AI is becoming a creative collaborator for filmmakers. This section navigates through how AI streamlines workflows, optimizes special effects, and contributes to the creation of visually stunning and innovative content.

5. Personalized Content Recommendations:

The personalized entertainment experience becomes a focus as AI algorithms analyze user preferences, viewing habits, and content consumption patterns. Recommender systems powered by AI are explored for their role in tailoring content suggestions across streaming platforms, ensuring that users discover and engage with content that aligns with their tastes.

6. AI and Augmented Reality (AR) Experiences:

As entertainment continues to embrace augmented reality, this section explores how AI enhances AR experiences. From interactive storytelling to immersive gaming overlays, AI-driven AR applications are creating novel and engaging forms of entertainment. The mid section unveils how AI contributes to the seamless integration of virtual elements into the real world.

7. Creative Collaborations with AI:

The chapter delves into how AI is not only a tool for creators but a collaborator in the creative process. AI-generated art, writing, and design are explored as mediums where human-AI collaborations lead to innovative and boundary-pushing creations. This section unravels the evolving role of AI in fostering creativity and expanding the horizons of artistic expression.

As we draw the chapter to a close, it becomes evident that AI is not merely a technological tool in entertainment; it is a catalyst for innovation, personalization, and new creative frontiers. The intersection of AI and entertainment is a dynamic space where technology enhances, augments, and sometimes even leads the creative process.

This underscores the transformative impact of AI in gaming, content creation, and personalized experiences. From virtual characters that learn and adapt to user preferences to AI-generated music that sets the tone for immersive storytelling, the possibilities are vast and continually expanding.

In conclusion, this chapter envisions a future where AI's role in entertainment continues to evolve, pushing the boundaries of what is possible. As technology advances and creative industries embrace AI, the landscape of entertainment will be shaped by a synergy of human ingenuity and machine intelligence. In the subsequent chapters, we will delve deeper into specific applications, emerging trends, and the overarching implications of AI in the ever-evolving world of entertainment.

AI and the Job Landscape - Opportunities and Challenges

The integration of Artificial Intelligence (AI) into the workforce has ushered in a new era in the job landscape, marked by both opportunities and challenges. "AI and the Job Landscape: Opportunities and Challenges," embarks on a comprehensive exploration of how AI is reshaping employment dynamics. From the creation of new job opportunities to the transformation of existing roles, this chapter delves into the multifaceted impact of AI on the world of work.

The introduction sets the stage by acknowledging the transformative potential of AI in enhancing productivity, automating tasks, and fostering innovation. However, it also recognizes the concerns surrounding job displacement, shifts in skill requirements, and the imperative for adaptive strategies in the face of AI-driven changes.

1. AI-Driven Job Creation:

The mid section opens with a positive perspective, examining how AI contributes to job creation. AI technologies fuel the growth of new industries, including data science, machine learning engineering, and AI ethics consulting. This section explores how the demand for skilled professionals in these emerging fields presents novel opportunities for the workforce.

2. Job Transformation and Skill Evolution:

The chapter navigates through the transformation of existing jobs due to AI integration. Tasks that are routine and repetitive become candidates for automation, prompting a shift in skill requirements. The mid section unravels how reskilling and upskilling initiatives become crucial for employees to remain relevant in the evolving job landscape.

3. AI and Human-AI Collaboration:

Human-AI collaboration emerges as a key theme, illustrating how AI technologies augment human capabilities. This section explores scenarios where AI acts as a collaborative partner, handling mundane tasks and allowing human workers to focus on more complex, creative, and decision-intensive aspects of their roles. The mid section unfolds the potential for synergistic relationships between humans and AI.

4. Impact on Routine and Manual Jobs:

Acknowledging the concerns around job displacement, the chapter delves into the impact of AI on routine and manual jobs. Automation technologies may replace certain repetitive tasks, raising questions about the future of jobs in manufacturing, logistics, and other sectors. The mid section explores the need for strategic workforce planning and inclusive policies to address potential job disruptions.

5. AI in Entrepreneurship and Small Businesses:

The mid section explores how AI technologies empower entrepreneurs and small businesses. AI-driven tools for market analysis, customer engagement, and operational efficiency offer accessible solutions that can level the playing field. This section highlights the democratizing effect of AI, enabling smaller entities to compete in a digitally transformed business landscape.

6. Ethical Considerations in AI Employment:

Ethical considerations take center stage as the chapter navigates through issues such as bias in AI algorithms, privacy concerns, and the responsible use of AI in employment decisions. The mid section emphasizes the importance of establishing ethical frameworks and guidelines to ensure fair and equitable AI integration in the workplace.

7. Global Perspectives on AI and Jobs:

The global dimension of AI's impact on jobs is explored, recognizing that the challenges and opportunities vary across regions. The chapter examines how different countries approach AI adoption, address workforce transitions, and foster international collaboration to navigate the evolving job landscape. As we conclude this exploration of AI and the job landscape, it becomes evident that the integration of AI is a transformative force that necessitates a proactive and adaptive approach. The mid section has unveiled a nuanced perspective, acknowledging both the opportunities and challenges inherent in the AI-driven evolution of the workforce. In conclusion, the chapter underscores the importance of a holistic approach to AI and employment. It emphasizes the need for continuous learning, reskilling, and upskilling to equip the workforce with the competencies required in the AI era. Moreover, ethical considerations must guide the responsible deployment of AI technologies, ensuring that the benefits are widespread and that potential drawbacks are mitigated. The job landscape is undergoing a profound shift, and embracing the opportunities presented by AI requires collaboration among governments, businesses, and educational institutions. As we move forward, the challenge is not merely adapting to AI but leveraging its potential to create a future where technology and human ingenuity coalesce to redefine the nature of work. In subsequent chapters, we will delve deeper into specific industries, policy considerations, and the overarching societal implications of AI integration in the job landscape.

The Future of AI - Emerging Technologies

As the landscape of Artificial Intelligence (AI) continues to evolve, the exploration of emerging technologies becomes paramount in understanding the trajectory of AI's future. "Emerging Technologies: The Future of AI," embarks on a journey to unravel the innovative advancements that are shaping the next frontier of AI. From quantum computing to neuro-inspired algorithms, this chapter delves into the transformative potential of cutting-edge technologies that will redefine the boundaries of what AI can achieve.

The introduction sets the stage by recognizing the rapid pace of technological innovation and the dynamic interplay between various emerging technologies. It underscores the significance of staying abreast of these developments to grasp the full spectrum of possibilities that will shape the future landscape of AI.

1. Quantum Computing and AI: Revolutionizing Processing Power:

It is amazing that an exploration of how quantum computing stands as a game-changer for AI. Quantum computers, with their ability to process vast datasets and perform complex calculations exponentially faster than classical computers, hold the potential to revolutionize AI algorithms. This section unravels the implications of quantum computing in optimizing machine learning models, solving complex problems, and unlocking new frontiers in AI research.

2. Neuromorphic Computing: Inspired by the Brain's Architecture:

Neuromorphic computing takes center stage as this section delves into technologies inspired by the brain's architecture. Mimicking neural networks, these systems aim to bring about more efficient and brain-like processing. The section explores how neuromorphic computing can lead to advancements in AI that excel at tasks requiring human-like perception, learning, and decision-making.

3. Explainable AI: Enhancing Transparency and Trust:

Transparency and interpretability in AI models become crucial focal points in this section. As AI systems become increasingly complex, the need for explainability grows. Emerging technologies that prioritize explainable AI (XAI) aim to demystify the decision-making process of AI algorithms. The mid section navigates through the importance of transparent AI models in building trust and facilitating wider adoption across industries.

4. Edge AI: Decentralized Intelligence for Real-time Processing:

The chapter explores how Edge AI represents a shift from centralized cloud computing to decentralized processing at the edge of the network. This technology enables real-time data analysis and decision-making, reducing latency and enhancing efficiency. The mid section discusses applications of Edge AI in various sectors, from healthcare to autonomous vehicles, and its potential to reshape the way AI interacts with the physical world.

5. Generative AI: Creating New Realities:

The realm of generative AI, where machines possess the ability to create novel content autonomously. From generating realistic images to creating entire paragraphs of text, generative AI models are at the forefront of creative applications. This section explores the potential of generative AI in fields such as art, design, and content creation, as well as the ethical considerations surrounding its use.

6. Blockchain and AI: Securing Trust and Accountability:

The intersection of blockchain and AI is explored as a means to enhance security, trust, and accountability in AI systems. Blockchain's decentralized and tamper-resistant nature can address concerns related to data privacy, bias, and the integrity of AI-generated outcomes. The mid section discusses how the marriage of blockchain and AI technologies can pave the way for more transparent and secure AI implementations.

7. Biotechnology and AI Integration: Advancing Healthcare and Beyond:

The convergence of biotechnology and AI takes center stage as the mid section navigates through the advancements in healthcare and beyond. From personalized medicine to genetic research, the integration of AI with biotechnology holds the promise of transformative breakthroughs. This section explores the potential of AI to analyze vast biological datasets, accelerate drug discovery, and revolutionize healthcare delivery.

As we conclude this exploration of emerging technologies and the future of AI, it becomes clear that the convergence of these cutting-edge advancements will redefine the possibilities of what AI can achieve. The mid section has unveiled a dynamic landscape, where quantum computing, neuromorphic architectures, explainable AI, Edge computing, generative models, blockchain integration, and the synergy with biotechnology collectively shape the trajectory of AI's future.

In conclusion, the chapter underscores the importance of interdisciplinary collaboration and continued exploration to unlock the full potential of emerging technologies. The synergy between AI and these innovations holds the key to addressing complex challenges and unlocking new realms of possibilities across industries. As we look ahead, the future of AI is not just about automation and efficiency but about pushing the boundaries of what is conceivable, creating intelligent systems that can augment human capabilities and contribute to the betterment of society.

In the subsequent chapters, we will delve deeper into the practical applications, ethical considerations, and societal impacts of these emerging technologies. The journey into the future of AI is one marked by innovation, exploration, and the collective effort to harness the full potential of these transformative advancements.

AI in Architecture

Revolutionizing Creative and Secure Building Plans

The fusion of Artificial Intelligence (AI) and architecture has ushered in a new era of innovation and efficiency in the design and planning of buildings. As architects grapple with increasingly complex challenges, AI emerges as a powerful ally, transforming the creative process and enhancing the security aspects of architectural designs. This article delves into the myriad ways in which AI is reshaping architecture, from generative design to sustainable practices, ultimately redefining the future of the built environment.

Generative Design: Redefining Creativity

At the heart of AI's impact on architecture is generative design, a process that leverages algorithms to explore countless design possibilities based on specified parameters.

Architects input their design goals, constraints, and preferences, and AI algorithms generate a plethora of potential solutions. This not only expedites the design phase but also pushes the boundaries of creativity by presenting architects with unconventional and innovative options.

1. Design Exploration Beyond Human Capacity:

AI's ability to process vast datasets and analyze intricate patterns allows it to explore design possibilities far beyond human capacity. Architects can now consider a myriad of factors simultaneously, including site conditions, environmental impact, and user preferences, leading to more holistic and innovative designs.

2. Rapid Iterations for Optimal Solutions:

Traditional design processes often involve time-consuming iterations. AI accelerates this cycle by swiftly generating and evaluating numerous design alternatives. Architects can efficiently refine and optimize their plans, ensuring that the final design aligns with project goals and constraints.

3. Enhancing Sustainability in Architecture:

Sustainability is a paramount concern in contemporary architecture. AI contributes by analyzing environmental data to propose designs that optimize energy efficiency, maximize natural light, and minimize environmental impact. The integration of sustainable practices becomes not only feasible but also intrinsic to the generative design process.

Security in Architectural Planning: A Collaborative Approach

Beyond creativity, AI plays a crucial role in enhancing the security aspects of architectural planning. By addressing concerns related to structural integrity, safety standards, and risk mitigation, AI ensures that architectural designs prioritize the well-being of occupants and adhere to regulatory requirements.

1. Structural Analysis and Safety Standards:

AI facilitates advanced structural analysis, evaluating the stability and safety of building designs. By simulating various load conditions and potential stresses, architects can preemptively identify vulnerabilities and optimize designs to meet or exceed safety standards. This not only ensures the longevity of structures but also safeguards against potential hazards.

2. Predictive Analytics for Risk Mitigation:

The integration of predictive analytics in architectural planning enhances risk mitigation strategies. AI algorithms analyze historical data, environmental conditions, and local risks to predict potential challenges such as flooding, earthquakes, or extreme weather events. Architects can then design structures that are resilient to these challenges, promoting long-term security.

3. Compliance with Building Codes and Regulations:

AI assists architects in navigating the complex landscape of building codes and regulations. By continuously updating databases with evolving standards, AI ensures that architectural designs remain compliant with local and international regulations. This proactive approach minimizes the risk of legal challenges and ensures that projects proceed smoothly through regulatory processes.

Real-world Applications: Showcasing AI's Impact

1. The Edge of Creativity: Zaha Hadid Architects and AI:

Zaha Hadid Architects, renowned for groundbreaking designs, collaborated with AI researchers to explore the possibilities of generative design. By employing machine learning algorithms, they generated intricate and fluid designs for a conceptual tower. This collaboration demonstrated how AI can push architectural boundaries, inspiring new possibilities that fuse human ingenuity with computational creativity.

2. Autodesk's Generative Design for AEC Industry:

Autodesk, a leader in architectural software, has introduced generative design tools specifically tailored for the Architecture, Engineering, and Construction (AEC) industry. This platform enables architects to harness AI for creating optimal designs that balance multiple objectives, from structural integrity to sustainability. The result is a collaborative approach where AI augments human expertise in the pursuit of innovative and secure architectural solutions.

Challenges and Ethical Considerations

As AI becomes an integral part of architectural practices, it is essential to address challenges and ethical considerations. The reliance on algorithms raises questions about transparency, accountability, and the potential bias embedded in AI models. Architects must navigate these complexities and ensure that AI is a tool for inclusive and ethical design practices.

Shaping the Future of Architecture

The marriage of AI and architecture holds immense promise for the future of the built environment. From unleashing unparalleled creativity through generative design to fortifying security aspects with predictive analytics, AI is reshaping how architects approach their craft. The real-world applications showcased by industry leaders exemplify the transformative potential of AI in fostering a collaborative and innovative architectural landscape.

As architects continue to embrace AI, it is imperative to strike a balance between technological advancement and ethical considerations. By harnessing the full potential of AI, architects can not only redefine the aesthetics of our surroundings but also prioritize safety, sustainability, and inclusivity in the architectural endeavors that shape the cities of tomorrow. The synergy between human creativity and machine intelligence holds the key to unlocking unprecedented possibilities in the field of architecture.

AI in Compliance Checking

Ensuring Precision in Critical Life Sciences and Healthcare Domains

In the ever-evolving landscape of life sciences and healthcare, where precision and adherence to quality standards are paramount, Artificial Intelligence (AI) is playing a pivotal role in compliance checking. The integration of AI technologies in these critical domains goes beyond mere automation; it ensures a level of accuracy, efficiency, and consistency that is essential for safeguarding human well-being.

This chapter explores the applications, benefits, and the transformative impact of AI in compliance checking across life sciences and healthcare sectors.

1. Life Sciences: Elevating Research and Development

a. Drug Discovery and Development:

AI is revolutionizing the drug discovery and development process. In compliance checking, AI algorithms can meticulously analyze vast datasets related to drug interactions, chemical structures, and regulatory requirements.

This not only expedites the identification of potential compounds but also ensures that the discovered drugs adhere to stringent quality and safety standards.

b. Regulatory Compliance in Clinical Trials:

Ensuring compliance with regulatory standards is crucial in clinical trials. AI streamlines the process by automating the review of protocols, patient data, and documentation. This not only reduces the likelihood of errors but also expedites the approval process, bringing life-saving treatments to patients faster while maintaining the highest standards of compliance.

2. Healthcare: Enhancing Patient Safety and Care

a. Medical Diagnosis and Imaging:

In healthcare, AI is transforming the field of medical diagnosis and imaging. AI algorithms, trained on vast datasets, assist healthcare professionals in identifying anomalies and potential issues in medical images. Compliance checking in this context involves ensuring that diagnostic procedures align with established protocols, minimizing the risk of oversight and optimizing patient care.

b. Electronic Health Records (EHR) Compliance:

The management of Electronic Health Records (EHR) is a critical aspect of healthcare operations. AI-powered systems can conduct comprehensive audits of EHRs, ensuring compliance with privacy regulations, data integrity, and accessibility standards. This not only enhances the security of patient information but also facilitates seamless interoperability across healthcare systems.

3. Quality Assurance: A Pillar of Reliability

a. Manufacturing Processes in Pharmaceuticals:

In pharmaceutical manufacturing, where product quality is non-negotiable, AI ensures compliance with Good Manufacturing Practice (GMP) standards. AI-driven systems monitor production processes, analyze data in real-time, and flag any deviations from quality parameters. This proactive approach minimizes the risk of defects and ensures that pharmaceutical products meet the highest quality standards.

b. Ensuring Product Safety in Medical Devices:

AI contributes to compliance checking in the manufacturing of medical devices by meticulously inspecting product designs and production processes. This includes the verification of safety features, adherence to regulatory requirements, and the overall reliability of the medical devices. The result is a streamlined manufacturing process that prioritizes product safety and efficacy.

4. Benefits of AI in Compliance Checking

a. Accuracy and Consistency:

AI excels in delivering accurate and consistent results. In compliance checking, this means that every aspect of processes, from clinical trials to manufacturing, is subjected to precise scrutiny. The elimination of human errors and variations ensures a higher level of compliance and reliability.

b. Speed and Efficiency:

The speed at which AI processes and analyzes data is unparalleled. This acceleration is particularly beneficial in compliance checking, where timely adherence to regulations is critical. AI expedites tasks such as document review, data analysis, and protocol assessments, reducing the time required for compliance checks.

c. Continuous Monitoring and Improvement:

AI's capability for continuous monitoring allows for real-time compliance checks throughout processes. Any deviations or anomalies can be promptly addressed, contributing to a dynamic and responsive approach to compliance. Moreover, AI systems can learn and adapt, continually improving their ability to identify and address compliance issues.

5. Challenges and Ethical Considerations

As with any technology, the integration of AI in compliance checking is not without challenges and ethical considerations. Ensuring transparency, addressing biases in algorithms, and safeguarding patient privacy are paramount concerns. Ethical frameworks must guide the development and deployment of AI systems in these critical domains to maintain trust and uphold the highest standards of integrity.

6. The Future Landscape: Toward Safer and More Efficient Practices

The integration of AI in compliance checking across life sciences and healthcare is not just a technological evolution; it is a paradigm shift toward safer, more efficient, and more reliable practices. As AI continues to advance, the future landscape holds the promise of even more sophisticated applications, including predictive compliance analytics, personalized treatment plans, and enhanced patient outcomes.

In conclusion, AI's role in compliance checking is a testament to its transformative impact on ensuring precision and adherence to quality standards in critical life sciences and healthcare domains. The synergy between human expertise and AI capabilities is shaping a future where compliance is not just a checkbox but a dynamic, data-driven, and patient-centric approach to delivering the highest standards of care and well-being.

Cautions and Concerns - Unraveling the Risks

As Artificial Intelligence (AI) continues to permeate diverse facets of our lives, from healthcare to finance and beyond, it is imperative to navigate the landscape with a discerning eye. "Cautions and Concerns - Unraveling the Risks," delves into the potential pitfalls and challenges associated with the widespread adoption of AI technologies. While AI offers unprecedented benefits, understanding and addressing its inherent risks is crucial to fostering responsible development and deployment.

The introduction sets the stage by acknowledging the transformative power of AI and the necessity of a balanced perspective. It highlights the ethical, societal, and technical concerns that underscore the need for cautious and informed approaches to AI integration.

1. Ethical Considerations: Navigating the Moral Compass of AI

a. Bias and Fairness:

One of the foremost concerns in AI is the perpetuation of bias. AI algorithms, often trained on historical data, can inherit and perpetuate societal biases, leading to discriminatory outcomes. This section explores the challenges of mitigating bias in AI models and the ethical imperative of ensuring fairness across diverse user groups.

b. Transparency and Accountability:

Transparency in AI decision-making processes is crucial for building trust. However, many AI algorithms, particularly complex deep learning models, operate as "black boxes," making it challenging to interpret their decisions. The mid section navigates through the importance of transparency and the challenges associated with holding AI systems accountable for their actions.

2. Societal Impact: Balancing Progress and Responsibility

a. Job Displacement and Economic Disparity:

The rise of automation powered by AI raises concerns about job displacement and economic inequality. This section examines the potential impact on employment sectors, the need for reskilling programs, and the broader socioeconomic implications of AI-driven shifts in the job landscape.

b. Social Manipulation and Privacy Concerns:

AI's ability to analyze vast datasets for predictive purposes raises questions about privacy and the potential for social manipulation. The mid section unravels the challenges associated with protecting individual privacy in the era of AI and navigating the ethical boundaries of data utilization.

3. Technical Challenges: Navigating the Complexity of AI Systems

a. Security Risks and Vulnerabilities:

AI systems are susceptible to security risks, including adversarial attacks and vulnerabilities in the underlying algorithms. This section explores the technical challenges of securing AI systems and the potential consequences of malicious exploitation.

b. Explainability and Interpretability:

It delves into the technical intricacies of making AI systems explainable and interpretable. Achieving transparency in the decision-making process of complex models is a technical challenge that impacts not only user trust but also regulatory compliance.

4. Unintended Consequences: Anticipating and Addressing Unforeseen Outcomes

a. Unintended Bias and Discrimination:

Despite efforts to eliminate bias, unintended consequences may lead to discriminatory outcomes. This section explores scenarios where AI systems inadvertently perpetuate bias and the measures that can be taken to anticipate and address these unintended consequences.

b. Autonomous Systems and Decision-Making:

The introduction of AI into autonomous systems raises questions about the ethical and legal implications of AI-driven decision-making. The mid section navigates through the challenges of defining accountability and responsibility when autonomous systems make critical decisions.

As we conclude this exploration of cautions and concerns in the realm of AI, it becomes evident that a nuanced understanding of the risks is essential for responsible AI development and deployment. The ethical, societal, and technical challenges associated with AI, emphasizing the importance of vigilance and proactive measures to mitigate these risks.

In conclusion, the chapter underscores the need for interdisciplinary collaboration, ethical frameworks, and ongoing scrutiny in the development and deployment of AI technologies. While AI offers transformative potential, acknowledging and addressing its risks are integral to ensuring that it serves as a force for positive change rather than a source of unintended harm.

As we continue on the journey of AI integration, it is imperative to approach this technology with a holistic perspective, anticipating challenges, and collectively working towards solutions. The future of AI must be shaped by a commitment to responsible innovation, where the benefits of technological advancement are realized without compromising ethical principles, societal well-being, and individual rights. Subsequent chapters will delve into specific strategies, frameworks, and case studies that contribute to the responsible development and deployment of AI technologies.

Risks in Using AI in Military Armies

Artificial Intelligence (AI) has increasingly found its way into military applications, promising enhanced capabilities and efficiency. While the integration of AI in the military brings several advantages, it also raises significant risks and concerns. This exploration delves into the potential pitfalls and ethical considerations associated with leveraging AI technologies in military armies.

1. Autonomous Weapon Systems: The Challenge of Decision-Making

a. Lack of Human Oversight:

One of the primary risks in using AI in the military is the development of autonomous weapon systems that operate without direct human control. The absence of human oversight raises concerns about the potential for unintended consequences and the inability to assess the ethical implications of AI-driven decisions.

b. Ethical Dilemmas in Target Selection:

AI's role in target selection introduces ethical dilemmas. The algorithms used to identify targets may be prone to biases or errors, leading to the risk of civilian casualties or the targeting of non-combatants. The challenge lies in ensuring that AI-driven decisions align with international humanitarian law and ethical norms.

2. Cybersecurity Vulnerabilities: A Battlefield in the Digital Realm

a. Target for Cyber Attacks:

AI systems in military applications are susceptible to cyber attacks. Malicious actors may attempt to manipulate or compromise AI algorithms, leading to potential disruptions in communication, intelligence, and strategic decision-making. Securing AI systems against cyber threats is a critical challenge.

b. Data Integrity and Manipulation:

The reliance on vast datasets for training AI models introduces the risk of data manipulation. If adversaries can infiltrate or manipulate the training data, it may result in distorted decision-making by AI systems, potentially impacting mission success and overall military operations.

3. Ethical and Moral Implications: Navigating the Gray Areas

a. Accountability for AI-Driven Actions:

Determining accountability for actions taken by AI systems poses a significant ethical challenge. In the event of errors or unintended consequences, attributing responsibility becomes complex, raising questions about legal and ethical accountability.

b. Unintended Consequences and Escalation:

The use of AI in military operations carries the risk of unintended consequences and escalation. The speed and autonomy of AI-driven decision-making may lead to rapid and unforeseen developments on the battlefield, potentially increasing the risk of conflict escalation.

4. Strategic and Geopolitical Concerns: Balancing Power Dynamics

a. AI Arms Race:

The pursuit of advanced AI capabilities by different nations may lead to an AI arms race. This competition for technological dominance raises concerns about the destabilizing effects of an unregulated and accelerated development of military AI technologies.

b. Deterioration of Human-Machine Relations:

The reliance on AI in military operations may lead to a deterioration of human-machine relations. Trust in AI systems is paramount, and any loss of confidence in the technology's reliability may impact the effectiveness of military strategies.

5. Secrecy and Lack of Transparency: Impeding Accountability

a. Opaque Decision-Making Processes:

The lack of transparency in the decision-making processes of AI systems used in the military can impede accountability. Understanding how AI algorithms arrive at certain decisions is crucial for ensuring compliance with international laws and ethical standards.

b. Limited Explainability in AI Models:

AI models, particularly complex deep learning algorithms, often lack explainability. The inability to explain how AI systems reach specific conclusions or recommendations poses challenges in justifying military actions and undermines transparency.

The integration of AI in military armies brings with it a myriad of risks that extend beyond the traditional challenges of warfare. Ethical, legal, and strategic considerations must be carefully navigated to ensure that the benefits of AI in military applications are realized without compromising human rights, international norms, and global stability.

As military forces continue to adopt AI technologies, it becomes imperative to establish robust regulatory frameworks, international agreements, and ethical guidelines that govern the development and deployment of AI in the military domain.

Striking a balance between technological advancement and responsible use is essential to harnessing the potential of AI while minimizing the associated risks. The evolving landscape of military AI requires ongoing scrutiny, ethical reflection, and a commitment to ensuring that these technologies serve humanity rather than pose existential threats.

Navigating the Ethical Maze - Guidelines for AI Development

In the ever-expanding landscape of Artificial Intelligence (AI), the ethical dimensions of AI development have become paramount. "Navigating the Ethical Maze: Guidelines for AI Development," is a comprehensive exploration of the ethical considerations that should guide the design, deployment, and impact assessment of AI technologies. This chapter delves into the evolving ethical landscape, presenting guidelines that aim to foster responsible AI development while minimizing potential risks and pitfalls.

The introduction establishes the critical importance of ethical considerations in AI development. It recognizes the multifaceted challenges posed by AI technologies and the need for a robust ethical framework to ensure that AI serves humanity's best interests.

1. Ethical Principles for AI Development: A Foundation for Responsible Innovation

a. Transparency and Explainability:

Transparency is a cornerstone of ethical AI development. Developers should prioritize creating AI systems with explainable decision-making processes. This section explores the importance of providing clear explanations for AI-driven decisions, fostering user trust, and enabling accountability.

b. Fairness and Avoidance of Bias:

Ensuring fairness in AI systems is paramount. Developers must actively identify and mitigate biases in datasets and algorithms. This section navigates through the challenges of addressing bias in AI, emphasizing the importance of fair and equitable outcomes across diverse user groups.

2. User Privacy and Data Protection:
Safeguarding Individual Rights

a. Informed Consent and Data Ownership:

Respecting user privacy requires obtaining informed consent and clearly defining data ownership. This section delves into the ethical considerations of collecting, storing, and processing user data, highlighting the importance of user agency and control over personal information.

b. Minimization of Data Collection:

Ethical AI development involves minimizing the collection of unnecessary user data. Developers should prioritize data minimization to reduce the potential for misuse and protect user privacy. This section explores strategies for responsibly managing and anonymizing data.

3. Human-Centric Design: Prioritizing Human Well-being

a. Human Rights Impact Assessments:

Integrating human rights impact assessments into AI development processes is crucial. This section explores the ethical imperative of evaluating potential societal impacts and ensuring that AI technologies do not infringe on fundamental human rights.

b. Accessibility and Inclusivity:

Ethical AI development requires a commitment to accessibility and inclusivity. Developers should strive to create AI systems that are accessible to diverse user populations, including individuals with disabilities. This section outlines principles for designing inclusive AI interfaces and functionalities.

4. Accountability and Governance: Upholding Responsibility

a. Clear Lines of Accountability:

Establishing clear lines of accountability is an ethical imperative in AI development. Developers, organizations, and stakeholders must understand their roles and responsibilities. This section explores the challenges of defining accountability in complex AI ecosystems.

b. Robust Governance Frameworks:

Ethical AI development necessitates the establishment of robust governance frameworks. This section outlines the key components of effective governance, including adherence to ethical guidelines, regular audits, and collaboration with regulatory bodies. As we conclude this exploration of ethical guidelines for AI development, it becomes evident that responsible innovation is essential for the sustainable and positive impact of AI technologies on society. The mid section has unraveled the multifaceted ethical considerations, providing a roadmap for developers, organizations, and policymakers to navigate the intricate ethical maze of AI.

In conclusion, the chapter emphasizes the dynamic nature of AI ethics, calling for continuous adaptation to evolving challenges and considerations. Ethical AI development is not a static goal but a journey marked by ongoing reflection, collaboration, and a commitment to prioritizing the well-being of individuals and society at large.

Moving forward, the ethical guidelines outlined in this chapter serve as a foundation for fostering a culture of responsibility in AI development. By integrating these principles into the fabric of AI innovation, we can collectively work towards an AI landscape that aligns with human values, respects individual rights, and contributes to a more inclusive and equitable future. Subsequent chapters will further explore case studies, best practices, and emerging trends in the ethical development of AI, ensuring a holistic and forward-looking approach to the responsible use of this transformative technology.

The Road Ahead - Balancing Progress and Responsibility

As we stand at the intersection of technological advancement and ethical considerations, "The Road Ahead: Balancing Progress and Responsibility," navigates the evolving landscape of Artificial Intelligence (AI). This chapter serves as a compass, guiding us through the challenges, opportunities, and ethical imperatives that shape the future of AI. With a focus on striking a balance between progress and responsibility, we embark on a journey to explore the path forward in harnessing the transformative potential of AI while safeguarding human values and societal well-being.

The introduction sets the stage by acknowledging the rapid pace of AI development and the critical need for a forward-looking approach that aligns technological progress with ethical considerations. It recognizes the inherent tension between the desire for innovation and the responsibility to ensure that AI benefits humanity.

1. Ethical Innovation: Harmonizing Technological Progress with Human Values

a. Iterative Ethical Design:

The road ahead demands an iterative approach to ethical design. This section explores the concept of embedding ethics into the development life cycle, ensuring that ethical considerations evolve alongside technological advancements.

b. Human-Centric AI:

The future of AI lies in human-centric design principles. This section delves into the importance of prioritizing human well-being, inclusivity, and user empowerment in AI systems, fostering a symbiotic relationship between technology and humanity.

2. Collaboration and Multidisciplinary Engagement:

a. Stakeholder Collaboration:

Ethical AI development requires collaboration among diverse stakeholders, including developers, policymakers, ethicists, and the general public. This section explores the benefits of fostering open dialogue and partnerships to address ethical challenges collectively.

b. Multidisciplinary Teams:

The complexity of AI challenges demands the involvement of multidisciplinary teams. This section advocates for diverse perspectives, incorporating expertise from fields such as ethics, sociology, psychology, and law to ensure a holistic approach to AI development.

3. Education and Ethical Literacy: Empowering Stakeholders

a. Ethics Education for Developers:

Ethical literacy is paramount in the development community. This section discusses the importance of integrating ethics education into the training of AI developers, empowering them to navigate ethical considerations effectively.

b. Public Awareness and Engagement:

A well-informed public plays a pivotal role in shaping the ethical trajectory of AI. This section explores strategies for raising public awareness, fostering a greater understanding of AI, and engaging the general populace in ethical discussions.

4. Regulatory Frameworks: Striking a Balance

a. Agile Regulatory Approaches:

The regulatory landscape must adapt to the dynamic nature of AI technologies. This section advocates for agile regulatory frameworks that balance the need for oversight with the flexibility required for innovation.

b. International Collaboration:

Ethical considerations transcend national boundaries. This section explores the importance of international collaboration in crafting ethical guidelines and regulatory standards that can harmonize the responsible development and deployment of AI globally.

As we conclude this exploration of the road ahead in balancing progress and responsibility in AI, it becomes evident that the journey requires a collective commitment from all stakeholders. The mid section has unraveled key strategies and principles that can guide us toward a future where AI not only advances technological frontiers but does so responsibly, ethically, and with a deep appreciation for human values.

In conclusion, the chapter emphasizes the ongoing nature of the ethical AI journey. Striking the right balance between progress and responsibility is not a one-time achievement but a continuous effort that demands adaptability, collaboration, and a dedication to the ethical evolution of AI technologies.

As we navigate the road ahead, it is crucial to view AI as a tool that should serve humanity's best interests. By prioritizing ethical innovation, fostering collaboration, empowering stakeholders through education, and embracing adaptive regulatory frameworks, we can shape a future where AI becomes an enabler of positive societal transformation.

The road ahead in AI is an exciting yet challenging expedition. By embracing responsibility as an integral part of progress, we can ensure that the transformative power of AI is harnessed to build a future where technology aligns with human values, fosters inclusivity, and contributes to the betterment of society at large. Subsequent chapters will continue to explore emerging trends, case studies, and best practices that further illuminate the ethical roadmap for the future of AI.

What AI Head, Former Senior Data security at NIIA say

"Real life working and actual data helps you to take decisions faster and stay ahead of The Others!"

" It always helped us while working for security measures forcountry's top decorated people...

This is the only **KEY** *to the* **RICHEST** *that is easy, important and achievable for a common man!*

Kindly check both the books. This one and the one mentioned below if you want to choose Best AI Company to invest.

Early the fastest is proved when Stock market is a major concern

This first book shall introduce you to the fascinating world of A.I and what its all about in common man's terms.

Make you aware about true or false fears of artificial intelligence. It also deals with the the Myths and Myths busted, gives lot of examples in order to take advantage ethically of this great technological tornado.

Second book which is here –

>> Click here to know AI Future Ahead – 2032 <<

Throws the light on very important and crucial data which in my view very very costly if one needs to buy it in accordance with stock market of AI Product companies.

Many of us have missed the Bitcoin wave and repenting till now....

But here is the chance to ride another wealth wave called Artificial intelligence ... and companies promoting its products!!

- William James
    (AI Head, Former Senior Data security at NIA)

>> Click here to know AI Future Ahead – 2032 <<

ın order to Invest in the Right AI Company

- A Global Perspective on REAL Statistical data, Trends, and Future Growth

>> Click here to know AI Future Ahead – 2032 <<

GIFT FOR ALL

PEOPLE lost the best opportunity to make money in the BITCOIN WAVE

BUT

With the help of this ebook, you shall ride the bigger wave than Bitcoin for sure.

>> https://www.amazon.com/dp/B0CVFBBK85 <<

- *William James*
  (AI Head, Former Senior Data security at NIA)

www.ingramcontent.com/pod-product-compliance
Lightning Source LLC
LaVergne TN
LVHW051324050326
832903LV00031B/3350